BASIC POTTERY FOR THE STUDENT

BASIC POTTERY
FOR THE STUDENT

HAROLD E. THORP

LONDON / ALEC TIRANTI / 1969

TO
MARIE, ANN and JOHN

Printed and bound by Weatherbys Printers of Wellingborough.

1969 ALEC TIRANTI LTD., 72 CHARLOTTE STREET, LONDON WIP 2AJ

MADE AND PRINTED IN THE UNITED KINGDOM
(GB) SBN 85458 549/4

CONTENTS

INTRODUCTION

'I forget the daily worries and feel completely relaxed'—or on a Friday evening, 'It unwinds me for the week-end'. Such are the typical comments from pottery evening students. Having arrived at Heathrow Airport at nine in the morning from a business trip to America, one student was only half an hour late for his pottery that same evening. Such is the fascination of pottery. It is fascinating because it is truly creative. Its medium is of the earth, its fashioning is with the hands, and its responsiveness to touch allows of spontaneous and vital expression; it encourages an easy start, and yet is inexhaustible in its possibilities.

Pottery is both an art and a craft and provides therefore a necessary antidote to the superficialities and the high pressure atmosphere of our modern way of life. It is the 'truth' from the art aspect and the 'integrity' from the craft aspect of pottery, rather than the gimmickry of 'instant' materialism which, in the end, give real satisfaction.

In a simple way, therefore, this book attempts to provide outlines on methods of making, on design and decoration, and on technical background. It is intended for adult evening students and for teachers and students concerned with obtaining their school certificates or diplomas. Above all, it aims at indicating a basic approach and understanding necessary to enjoy the rewarding opportunities that pottery offers.

ACKNOWLEDGEMENTS

I wish to thank all those who have so kindly helped in making this book possible. In particular, Brigadier F. Pocock, O.B.E., M.C., whose encouragement helped me to get it in motion, Mr. Ronald G. Cooper who so generously revised the drawings and offered much useful comment and Mr. Alec Tiranti who so kindly and tirelessly carried out its production.

H.E.T.

Bexley, 1969

CHAPTER ONE

CLAY TO POTTERY

WHAT CLAY IS AND ITS PLASTIC NATURE

Clay is decomposed felspar, an hydrated compound of alumina and silica. Millions of years of weathering have gradually broken up granite rocks into particles of microscopic size, and during this natural process, water has combined chemically with each particle to form the clay crystal. The shape of this clay crystal is essentially flat or sheet-like and this accounts for the plastic nature of clay. Just as water between two sheets of glass will cause suction, so too does water, added between adjacent crystals of clay, cause the mass of damp clay to stick together. When clay is pushed into a shape, the millions of flat clay crystals remain in that shape. Clay then is plastic and perhaps the most amenable of all plastics since it can be readily shaped at room temperature without the need of heat.

PRIMARY CLAYS

Clays vary considerably in the degree of their plasticity and this is due largely to the crystal size of a particular clay. Granite that has decomposed *in situ*, produces clay with a large size crystal and consequently a comparatively less plastic nature. Such kaolins or china clays are known as primary clays. They are often found relatively pure, and are ideal for many industrial uses besides ceramics, such as in the making of paper, paint, linoleum, face powder, medicaments etc.

SECONDARY CLAYS

Secondary clays are those that are found away from the original site of decomposition. Movement of the earth's surface has caused rivers to take with them particles which, through friction and the gradual loss of heavier particles, have finally settled into beds of finer sized crystals of clay. Other finely divided impurities, particularly lime and iron, may well settle with the clay. Such secondary clays therefore, are much more plastic and vary considerably from one locality to another. Thus red clays contain a high proportion of finely divided iron, while ball clays, so named from a method of mining from the ground and dispatching in lumps or balls, are comparatively pure, and are the most plastic of all clays.

CLAY BODIES

This rich variety of clays and clay materials enables the potter to prepare 'clay bodies' to suit his particular requirements. A typical clay body might contain china clay, ball clay and flint. An increase in the ball clay content will make the body more plastic in use, but more ready to shrink and warp in the kiln. The higher the flint content, the less plastic would be the body in use, but the consequent increase in silica from the flint would make it more refractory, or able to withstand a higher temperature, without loss of shape, so that the end product would be harder. An earthenware body is a mixture of clays and clay materials which, although it may mature at say 1150 °C., is still porous. Beyond this temperature it would begin to melt or would be liable to crack on cooling. A stoneware body is a mixture of clays including some fluxing material such as felspar which, at maturing temperatures of from 1250 °C. to 1350 °C., produces dense and non-porous vitrified pottery. Similarly, bone ash and felspar in bone china, and felspar in porcelain bodies, produce the vitrification and translucent qualities in these kinds of pottery which, like stoneware, are dense and impervious to water.

GROG

A potter may prefer a smooth plastic body for making domestic ware but might well prefer a clay with a 'tooth' for larger pieces. For such work as casseroles, this 'tooth' could be obtained by the addition of fine sand but for large decorative ware, a coarse 'grog' or ground biscuit could be added. Grogged clay is of particular use in making large slab pots and tiles, as it 'opens' the body and so enables it to dry more evenly and fire with less chance of mishap. The addition of non plastic materials such as sand, flint or grog, makes for a biscuit body less mechanically strong than a denser plastic body would give, and a much higher temperature is required in the glost firing to mature it. Indeed, certain heavily grogged bodies are still porous at generally accepted stoneware temperatures of about 1300 °C. If it is not desirable to raise the firing temperature and if an impervious body is required, then a plastic clay may be added to lower the maturing temperature. If a warmer coloured body is required, then red clay with its iron content would be preferable, but ball clay could be used if the body colour must not be unduly altered.

From this brief indication of the behaviour of clays and clay materials at the potter's command, it can be seen just how over-whelming is the variety of choice. To be aware of this, is to have unlatched only one of the gates to the many fields of exciting exploration that make up the art of pottery.

BISCUIT POTTERY

Having fashioned a form in damp clay, it then remains at room temperature to allow most of the mechanically added water to dry out, with a consequent considerable shrinking in size. From a practical point of view it is well to remember that the maximum shrinkage occurs from the damp to the 'leather hard' state, which is, therefore, the appropriate time for the addition of handles, spouts etc. The form is then put into the kiln and the temperature is raised very slowly indeed, not more than 50 °C. per hour at first, to allow the remainder of the added water to change into steam and escape through some opening in the kiln. After the kiln has been allowed to continue its gradual rise in temperature, a dull red glow will be seen. This indicates a temperature of about 500 °C. and at this period the chemically combined water is driven off to change the clay into a new, hard and rock like material that is known as biscuit pottery. The higher the temperature the harder the biscuit becomes. Most studio potters fire ware to 900 °C. when the body is strong enough for handling and still very porous. This porous quality, achieved as the chemically combined water has been driven off to leave microscopic air channels, is of great use in facilitating the glazing process.

GLOST POTTERY

Biscuit pottery is coated with glaze by dipping, pouring, painting or by spraying a mechanical mixture of powdered glass ingredients suspended in water. The water is readily absorbed by the porous biscuit which sucks on a coating of glaze. This glazed form is then returned to the kiln and made red hot, say 1100 °C., to melt the powdered glaze into a molten liquid. On cooling, a hard shiny glass surface results. This higher temperature also causes the body to become more dense and less porous. Porous pottery, earthenware, requires a well fitting skin of glaze to make it watertight. Stoneware, however, is a sintered or 'glassy' body, and does not require glazing for this purpose. It is itself impervious, harder than steel, acid resistant, and is virtually a permanent material.

This surely is the intrinsic fascination of pottery making – that from a soft piece of clay a form can be readily fashioned, and then by subjecting it to burning in a kiln, can be changed into a rock-hard permanent material – pottery. Man in a matter of hours, has in effect, reversed the decomposition process performed by nature over millions of years, to return soft clay to something akin to its original stony nature.

ROCK ⟶ CLAY ⟶ POTTERY FLOW CHART

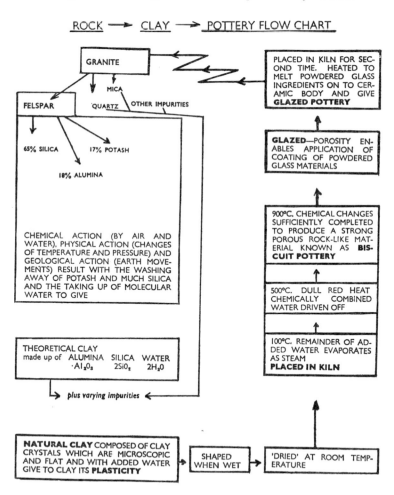

GRANITE

MICA

FELSPAR   QUARTZ   OTHER IMPURITIES

65% SILICA   17% POTASH

18% ALUMINA

CHEMICAL ACTION (BY AIR AND WATER), PHYSICAL ACTION (CHANGES OF TEMPERATURE AND PRESSURE) AND GEOLOGICAL ACTION (EARTH MOVEMENTS) RESULT WITH THE WASHING AWAY OF POTASH AND MUCH SILICA AND THE TAKING UP OF MOLECULAR WATER TO GIVE

THEORETICAL CLAY
made up of ALUMINA SILICA WATER
$\cdot Al_2O_3$ $2SiO_2$ $2H_2O$

plus varying impurities

NATURAL CLAY COMPOSED OF CLAY CRYSTALS WHICH ARE MICROSCOPIC AND FLAT AND WITH ADDED WATER GIVE TO CLAY ITS PLASTICITY

SHAPED WHEN WET

'DRIED' AT ROOM TEMPERATURE

100°C. REMAINDER OF ADDED WATER EVAPORATES AS STEAM
PLACED IN KILN

500°C. DULL RED HEAT CHEMICALLY COMBINED WATER DRIVEN OFF

900°C. CHEMICAL CHANGES SUFFICIENTLY COMPLETED TO PRODUCE A STRONG POROUS ROCK-LIKE MATERIAL KNOWN AS BISCUIT POTTERY

GLAZED—POROSITY ENABLES APPLICATION OF COATING OF POWDERED GLASS MATERIALS

PLACED IN KILN FOR SECOND TIME. HEATED TO MELT POWDERED GLASS INGREDIENTS ON TO CERAMIC BODY AND GIVE GLAZED POTTERY

CHAPTER TWO

PREPARATION OF CLAY, AND PINCHED POTS

Clay must be prepared before it can be successfully worked. It must be of a uniform texture if it is to respond willingly to the touch and not distort in firing, and it must be free from air pockets if it is not to explode in the kiln. There are clay mixing machines known as pugmills, which, if properly used, perform these tasks very well. Most potters however, prefer to prepare clay by hand and use one, or both, of two methods – spiralling and wedging.

Spiralling clay is similar to kneading dough. A lump of clay, tilted at 45° to the bench, is held with the right hand so that it is prevented from

1. The spiralling process

falling back onto the bench. The top edge is then folded towards the middle, and the movement is finished by pressing the middle onto the the bench. The clay is lifted with the left hand, slightly rotated clockwise, and the right hand then repeats the operation. For a large mass of clay, the left hand can cover the right hand to give increased power. This is an excellent method for mixing clays of different colours or consistencies.

Wedging is the traditional way of preparing clay, although often its meaning is not clearly demonstrated in practice. It is more than cutting a lump of clay into two and slamming one half down on the other. If the maximum effect is to be gained from the energy that this method demands, then a specific 'drill' is imperative. A 'wedge' of clay, inclining towards

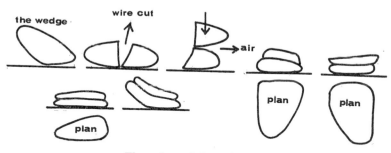

2. *The wedge and the wedging process*

the potter, is tapped onto the bench. A wire is then drawn almost vertically from bottom to top, to cut the wedge into two. The free, upper half, is then turned upwards and over so that the cut surfaces face the potter. The upper half, lightly held, is then raised above the potter's head and 'pulled' down with the full weight of the shoulders onto the *edge* of the mass of clay on the bench. This combined mass is then turned over away from the potter so that the bottom smooth surface is uppermost. It is turned through 90° so that the more pointed end faces the potter, lifted with the hands covering only the forward half of the base, and gently tapped into a wedge shape on the bench. The process is then repeated. The requirements of de-airing and mixing are satisfactorily achieved if the above procedure is rigidly followed. By bringing the upper mass down onto the near ridge of the wedge on the bench, the air is forced out as the two pieces of clay weld themselves together. This is, in fact, the explanation of the term 'wedging'. By rotating the clay through 90° alternately left and right to bring the 'point' forward, the folds are kept neat, and bring the joined mass into a ham shape. This minimises folds that are potential traps for air. So, too, does the reversing of the mass from bottom to top, produce two smooth surfaces which, when brought into contact, reduce the chances of trapping air. That wedging mixes the clay thoroughly is shown convincingly by simple mathematics. First two single layers are stacked together to make two, then by vertical cutting, each two layers are

14

brought together to make four. Each successive cut doubles the number of layers so that only twenty cuts are needed to produce over a million layers of clay. Having wedged the clay, it is then 'blocked' to a suitable shape by throwing it onto the bench. It is then ready for working. The correct working consistency of a piece of clay is dependent upon the method of making and the job in hand, but generally it is advisable to have the clay as damp as possible providing the form will retain its shape.

MAKING A PINCHED POT IN THE HAND

Any craft demands some knowledge of the behaviour of its material before a successful start can be made. A potter uses few tools but relies very much on his hands. He is particularly concerned at first therefore, with learning the 'feel of the clay'; with discovering just how responsive it is, in differing degrees of dampness, to every application of pressure. A pot, pinched in the hand, provides an excellent exercise for this exploration. Cut off a piece of clay and roll it firmly into a sphere a little smaller than

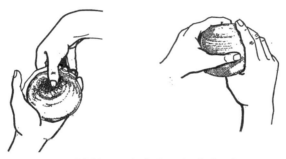

3, 4. Making a pinched pot in the hand

a tennis ball. Holding it in the palm of the left hand, insert the right thumb vertically into the middle, to within ⅜ in. of the base. Withdraw the thumb by twisting and replace it holding the clay uppermost. Starting at the base, press the middle fingers against the thumb, rotating the clay a little anti-clockwise at each even pressure. After every complete revolution, move the pressure slightly down from the base and continue until the edge is carefully finished. Holding the pot with both thumbs inside and fingers outside, gently tap the base flat onto the bench. Now repeat the pinching process from the base to the lip, as before, but with the base resting on the bench. Aim at maintaining an upright rather than an open shape and practice narrowing the form by 'pleating' the walls at 12 o'clock, or 6 o'clock, the outside pressures always dominating those from the inside. This will produce a control of the form which would otherwise inevitably drift towards opening wider. The pot can be finished by smoothing with the thumb and fingers and cutting textured patterns with the nails; or the finger indentations, similar to the marks from the planishing hammer in beaten metalwork, may well be satisfying by themselves. If allowed to dry to leather hardness, the surface could then be burnished by using any smooth implement, and, if desired, crisp-cut incisions, perhaps with a looped wire tool, could be made in the surface. When fired, such a pot would be best glazed on the inside only, to enhance the quality of the polished outside surface.

MAKING A PINCHED POT ON A BANDING WHEEL

Place a ball of clay 3in. to 4in. in diameter at the centre of the wheel head, and 'hammer' it with the tips of the thumbs held over the centre, whilst the vertical fingers support the outside of the mass. At each pressure, the wheel is simultaneously rotated anti-clockwise and very soon the process gives way to pinching the clay as described above. Having thinned the

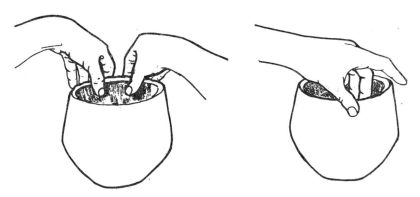

5, 6. Making a pinched pot on a banding wheel

walls to ¼ in. in thickness and 'pleated' them to arrive at the required shape, the rim, at least, should be sufficiently concentric to enable it to be finished by the same procedure as is used for a thrown pot. The wheel is spun anti-clockwise and the edge moistened with a sponge. The 'left-hand drill' process (see p.27) is then applied, followed by trimming the lip with a needle and shaping and sponging it as required. This final treatment to a pinched pot impresses vividly and demonstrates the inherent strength of a thrown lip which, like the rim of a cartwheel, holds the whole form together. Furthermore it provides, at an early stage, an introduction to the more complicated process of throwing.

CHAPTER THREE

COILED POTS

The following method of making a coiled pot is perhaps the most accurate and has the advantage that, in the final stages, an introduction is made to the shaping process in throwing, to finish off the rim of the pot.

MAKING THE BASE

1). Take a ball of clay 3in. in diameter in the left hand palm and hit it firmly in the centre with the heel of the right hand. Continue this and reverse the clay taking care not to thin the edges until the slab of clay is about half an inch in thickness.

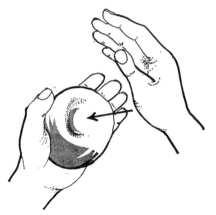

Figure 7

2). Place the clay on a clean, dry bench and beat it with the edge of the right hand to level the under surface of the clay. Move the clay to another dry part of the bench to prevent it sticking and gently tap it to make contact with the bench surface.

3). Slice the clay with a cutting frame set to give a thickness of about $\frac{3}{8}$ in. and remove the top waste.

4). Place this slice of clay of uniform thickness onto a banding wheel as near the centre of the wheel as possible and lightly tap it to bring it into contact with the wheel head.

18

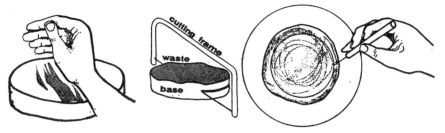

8-10. Flattening ball of clay for base; slicing off waste clay; trimming base

5). With a needle held firmly above the 3 o'clock position, rotate the wheel smoothly, lower the needle to just touch the clay at the required diameter and increase the pressure on the needle downwards to cut through to the wheel head. Remove the surplus edge.

MAKING A COIL

1). With the palms of the hands touching at the heels, hold a piece of clay about two inches in diameter. Gently holding the clay in the left hand, withdraw the right hand and return it sharply to hit the lower end of the clay. Slightly rotate the clay and repeat the process until a point is made. Reverse the clay and point the other end. These points ensure that no air will be trapped in the ends of the coils when they are rolled.

11. Pointing end of coil

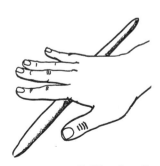

12. Rolling the coil

19

2). Holding this cigar shaped clay along the fingers of the left hand, hit it firmly with the outstretched fingers of the right hand, rotate it slightly, and repeat until a long cigar shape is formed.

3). Place this roll at the far side of the bench and with the heel of the hand resting on it, slowly and firmly move the clay to the finger tips. This operation, repeated five or six times, will produce a coil which 'feels' round.

4). Finish the coil by holding the hands almost in line with the length of clay and rolling backwards and forwards as far as the hand will allow from the little finger tip to the thumb base, and back, maintaining even contact all the time. If the clay is stiff, moisten the bench with a damp sponge to assist in producing a coil of uniform thickness.

FIXING THE FIRST COIL TO THE BASE

1). Place the middle of the coil on the base at 12 o'clock and gently bend each end towards 6 o'clock. Mitre the right end by cutting it with a needle and place the left hand end to overlap. Mark this end a little shorter, lift it from the base and mitre it.

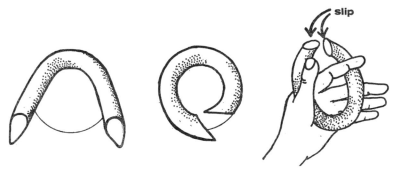

13-15. Bending coil; cutting it to size; holding it for joining with slip

2). Remove the coil from the base and hold it between the out-stretched thumb and three fingers of the left hand while the forefinger passes through the loop to support the inside of the two ends. Apply slip to each end and, fully overlapping them, press firmly together to expel any surplus slip and carefully model the join.

3). Position the coil on the base by pressing the four finger tips of each hand against the edge of the base at 12 o'clock and, rotating anti-clockwise

20

at each pressure, move the coil with the thumbs towards the fingers. 4). Continuing this process, move the thumb tips to a more horizontal position and to the top of the coil and so 'beat' the inside edge of the coil towards the base. At the second revolution, the clay should just make con-

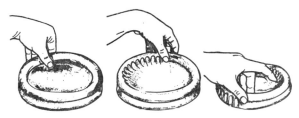

16-18. Positioning and 'beating' coil (two hands); modelling the outside of base coil

tact with the base so that the third revolution can produce a sliding action towards the centre of the base and the inside will then be smoothly finished. 5). Now, holding the fingers inside and the thumbs outside, both vertically at 6 o'clock, press the thumbs inwards and downwards ⅛ of an inch to model the outside of the coil to the base. The coil should now be accurately fixed to the base and all air excluded from the join. A beginner need never fear finding the base separated from the body, after firing, if this method is carefully followed.

FIXING SUBSEQUENT COILS

1). Cut, mark to size, join and position as for the first coil.
2). Model the inside similarly to the first coil taking care to support the outside adequately with vertically stretched fingers.
3). Model the outside by placing the four fingers of the right hand under the wheel head and pressing the thumb inwards and downwards towards the fingers that are against the inside wall at 5 o'clock. Aim at 'tacking'

19. Modelling the outside of subsequent coils

21

the coil for the first revolution and sliding the clay downwards for the second time round.

4). Holding the left hand at 11 o'clock and the right at 1 o'clock, with fingers vertical on the outside and thumbs on the inside, 'pleat' the clay to 12 o'clock while squeezing the fingers towards the thumbs. This method of evenly pinching the clay will cause the walls of the pot both to thin and rise. It provides an excellent practice in controlling the form of a pot which is otherwise inclined to grow into a sagging and purposeless shape, completely devoid of life.

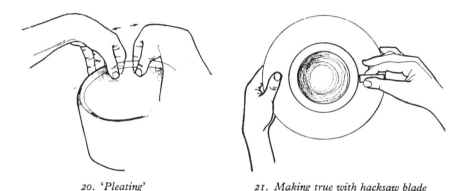

20. 'Pleating'   21. Making true with hacksaw blade

5). After fixing the third or fourth coil, scrape the walls with a piece of a large hacksaw blade held firmly at an angle and drawn upwards against the clay, supported by the fingers of the left hand.

6). Correct the accuracy of the shape of the pot by holding the blade, between the thumb and three fingers, against the clay, with the little finger acting as a gauge on the rim of the wheel head, while the left hand turns the wheel anti-clockwise about 30° at a time. Repeat 4 and 5 above as required.

FINISHING THE POT

1). Having spun the wheel head anti-clockwise with the left hand, take up the 'left-hand drill' position (p. 27) and squeeze a little water from a sponge onto the revolving rim. Holding a needle firmly against the left thumb and about a ¼ in. from the uneven top edge of the pot, slowly

22

allow it to rest against the clay and then increase the pressure to cut through the clay wall and 'prick' the inside finger. Lift upwards to remove the trimmed off waste.

2). Again with the 'left-hand drill', apply a damp sponge to press onto the rim and so smooth it off.

3). If desired, the edge can be thickened by replacing the sponge with the forefinger of the right hand so that the inside edge of the nail cuts in from the outside towards the inside of the rim. Sharp edges can be gently softened by applying the sponge.

4). Cut the pot off by drawing a tightly stretched wire between the base and wheel head.

Other more speedy methods of making coiled pots can be undertaken once a preliminary skill, such as the accurate method above provides, has been acquired. Rosemary Wren, who makes large coiled pots, uses a method of pinching coils into a triangular section. The pot is then built by thumbing the clay down on each side.

THE CONTINUOUS COILED METHOD

This method employs long coils of random length, that are modelled on in a spiral fashion. The coil can be rolled on the bench with less accuracy than that required by the first method, or 'rolled' vertically by the forward and backward squeezing of a mass of clay between the palms of the hands.

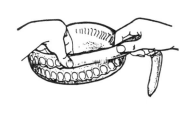

22. *Vertical rolling of coil*   23. *Modelling a continuous coil*

It is then held vertically with the right hand, while the left thumb models it to the base or previous part of the coil below, and the left hand fingers firmly support the outside. It is important to join the beginning and end of each coil very carefully. After every three or four rings, the inside wall

23

is smoothed and the outside wall modelled and smoothed, perhaps with a tool, to obtain the required shape. Pinching and pleating can also be used if necessary, and the rim can be finished by trimming and fixing a single coil.

SLABBED COILS

These can be used for large pots. A thick coil is held with one end clear of the bench while the opposite end is beaten with the lower edge of the

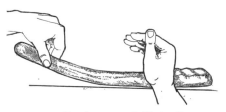

24. Beating out a slabbed coil

other hand held vertically. The clay is turned over and beaten on the other side. A length of clay, taken straight from a 2 in. diameter pugmill, can be treated in the same way, or slices of clay, about two inches in width, can be cut, with the aid of a straight edge, from a slab of clay. In all cases a suitable thickness is about $\frac{1}{2}$ in. These methods of building are very speedy, but as great care is needed in joining, they are best attempted only after considerable skill has been acquired by the accurate method.

COILED AND THROWN POTS

If carefully made, coiled pots can be finally shaped by the throwing process (p. 25). This enables a larger pot to be 'thrown' at a much earlier stage than could be achieved by the full throwing technique alone. For certain forms, especially large flat-based bowls (p. 44) this method compares favourably with direct throwing. It consists of making an accurate coiled pot on a bat, transferring it to the throwing wheel, and having centred it, finishing it by the shaping process as used in throwing. Before throwing, sufficient coils should be added to allow the squeezing process to produce the final form. For once a coiled pot is made wet, it requires to dry out somewhat before further coils can readily be added.

24

CHAPTER FOUR

THROWN POTS

'Throwing' is the method of making a pot on a potter's wheel. As the wheel revolves at speed, centrifugal force causes the clay on it to 'throw' outwards. It is the control of this force and movement that makes throwing so absorbing both to watch and to practise. It is accomplished in a space of minutes and so is capable of displaying the spontaneous feelings, choices and decisions, that a potter has to make. It is a unique hand process, and although it may well 'take ten years (and more!) to make a thrower', an initial effort, and understanding of the basic principles, brings early results of suprisingly worthwhile standard – especially if the attitude of 'making a dozen and hoping to save one' is adopted.

Take a ball of clay 3 in. in diameter, place it on the wheel head and tap it as near to the centre as possible. There are then three stages in the process, centring the clay on the wheel, opening it out at the base, and shaping it first into a cylinder and then into the final form. As with all hand skills, before touching the clay, the potter must be in the correct position, sitting or standing back from the wheel and then leaning the shoulders well up to the job. Rest the arms on the tray edge for support and rotate the wheel anti-clockwise at a fast speed of about 180 revolutions a minute. Wet the hands and the clay and holding the hands in a 'roof' position, press them firmly onto the clay to ensure that it adheres to the

| *25.* 'Roof' *position pressed onto wheel* | *26. Clay cleaned true at base by little fingers* | *27. Clay squeezed firmly as hands move upwards to make a cone* |

wheel head. Still holding the hands firmly, apply considerable pressure with the little fingers to clean the clay at the base, move the hands forward and slowly squeeze the clay upwards to form a cone, thus working up any irregularity to the apex. Next, hold the left hand so that the thumb is on top, then using the ball of the thumb gently persuade the clay off centre a little, and by pressing downwards, return the apex into a dome whilst gradually bringing into play pressures from the three lower fingers. Should the clay not be perfectly centred, the process can either be repeated or pressure can be supplied through the arm and wrist to the base of the left hand at 6 o'clock while the straightened right hand presses (or is pressed) in opposition at 2 or 3 o'clock. For as long as the clay remains a solid mass, the basic principle of centring lies in pressure or pressures being applied *against* the movement of the clay, and always directed to the centre of the wheel head. The final centred shape should be dome-like.

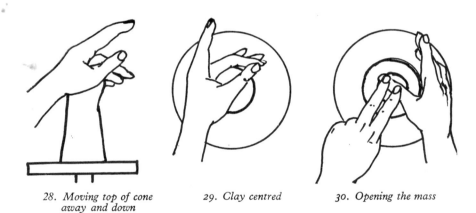

28. *Moving top of cone*   29. *Clay centred*   30. *Opening the mass*
   away and down

To open the centred mass, hold the right hand straight to touch the clay and wheel with the little finger at 3 o'clock. Place the thumb to discover the centre and then, with pressure from the first two fingers of the left hand on the right thumb, continue moving downwards into the centre of the clay until within ¼ in. of the wheel head. At this point, re-wetting the clay may well be necessary before proceeding to press the thumb outwards to the fingers at 3 o'clock and then pressing the fingers inwards against the thumb. Drawing this pressure a little upwards, the walls of the opened mass will now be even in thickness.

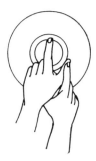

31. Shaping, squeezing clay between 'left hand drill'

Shaping of the clay now follows by employing the 'left-hand drill' process. This consists of pressing the pad of the second finger on the inside of the cylinder of clay at 5 o'clock and against the thumb supporting the outside of the clay at 5 o'clock. The thumb can be 'forced' to 6 o'clock by holding the right forefinger against it so that its pad touches the clay at 5 o'clock. Pressure between the inside and outside fingers at 5 o'clock is now applied and both hands are slowly raised simultaneously to squeeze the clay from the base upwards and so produce a growing cylinder. This process is repeated until the walls are of a suitable thickness, about a $\frac{1}{4}$ in., depending on the final form and the type of clay used. A coarser body may well demand a stouter thickness than one of finer texture. This basic 'left-hand drill' lends itself to variations. While the position of the left hand remains the same, the outside pressure, maintained in contact with the left hand by pressing against the left thumb, can take the form of the right forefinger, the knuckle of the forefinger crooked round its thumb,

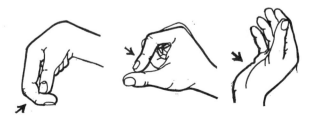

32. Stronger right hand positions for squeezing clay

27

a tool such as a bone or hacksaw blade held with the fingers and thumb, a kidney rubber or a sponge. For larger masses of clay yet further right hand positions can be employed according to the potter's individual preference. Yet whatever choice is made, the basic principle always applies: that the clay be squeezed between the inside and outside pressures always opposite to each other on the radius of the circle. Most potters prefer the 5 o'clock or 4 o'clock position, since at this point the clay wall, revolving anti-clockwise, is in fact moving away from the pressure and so receives more gentle treatment.

It is suggested that much practice at throwing cylinders is well worthwhile before attempting 'shaped curves'. Indeed, from the very beginning there is not only the excitement of acquiring technical control, but also the challenge of solving aesthetic problems as indicated in the chapter on design (p. 47).

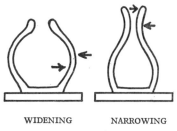

WIDENING   NARROWING

33. Vertical positions of pressures

In order to produce a curved or rounded form, all that is necessary is to raise either the inside or outside pressure slightly vertically above the other. Thus to produce a convex curve, the pressures, starting vertically opposite, adjust on their upward movement so that the lower pressure is from the inside. This forces the clay outwards. A neck or concave curve can then be formed by moving the inside pressure above the outside so that the last pressure applied to the moving clay is from the outside. If the

34, 35. Strong and light 'collaring'

28

pressures are then applied vertically opposite, a parallel neck can follow. Should the neck require narrowing, the process of 'collaring' can be employed. The pot is simply grasped between the two fingers and the thumbs of both hands held opposite to each other, and pressure is applied inwards and upwards. Since collaring forces the clay into shape rather than squeezes the clay into a new position, it is best followed with the squeezing process to maintain the strength of the form. All shapes are started by first making a cylinder, but in the case of bowls a curved based low cylinder

36. Dome; start of opening; base to size; cylinder; shape

is made and as the clay is drawn out it is necessary to retain a thicker section at the base in order to support the walls. With vertical pots it is important to throw them uniformly thick as near from the base as possible when a much more lively form is likely to follow. Often, if the bottom inch is cleaned with the thumb or edge of a tool, it is possible to cut the pot off the wetted wheel with a tightly stretched piece of stranded wire, so that the base requires no further attention except perhaps to 'fettle' lightly or clean the arris. Usually, however, the base, because it supports the clay above, should be thicker than required; later it can be 'turned' to enhance the character and 'feel' of the final form. The correct weight of a pot is dependent upon its form. A massive pot must not surprise one by feeling too light, nor should a finely thrown form appear unexpectedly heavy. Pots are usually of a size to invite handling, and this fondling and 'weighing' of them in the hands, is part of our aesthetic judgement. The weight of a pot must give a feeling of balance.

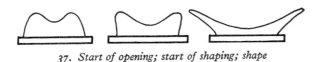

37. Start of opening; start of shaping; shape

This can be carried out, as in industry, on an horizontal lathe, but most studio potters simply place the pot upside down on the wheel head and trim the base when the clay is in the 'leather hard' state. Various methods and tools can be employed. A direct method is to damp slightly both the wheel head and rim of the pot and position it as near to the centre as possible. Revolve the wheel anti-clockwise, and holding a point or tool edge or finger, bring it closer to the pot until it makes a slight mark. If the mark is made at one point only, then the pot is too far from centre at this point. Accordingly, with the careful pressure of fingers and thumbs, move the pot slightly towards the centre. Check again until an even mark is made all round the form. Gently press the pot onto the wheel head and often the suction produced is sufficient to hold the pot firmly on to the wheel. It is safer however to carefully press two opposite pairs of small clay wads

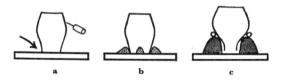

38. (a) Slightly dampen rim and wheelhead, and test for centrality as wheel revolves. (b) Four wads of clay pressed onto wheel and gently towards rim. (c) Clay chuck with clay wads

39. Cup head as chuck

firmly onto the wheel head and squeezing them downwards to just touch the pot's rim, and so ensure that the pot will not be shot off the revolving wheel. This must be carried out carefully as it is important not to deform the rim whose full circle gives so much strength to the finished pot. For this reason the practice of pressing thick coils of clay round the rim is best avoided. With narrow necked pots it is necessary to make a chuck into which the neck fits for protection, the pot resting on the stronger shoulder. The chuck can be made by throwing a thick ring of clay and allowing it to harden or by turning from a solid mass of firm clay. A cup head, if available, can be utilized by 'padding' it with a coil of clay and then turning it true. With most chuck methods it is advisable to add four small wads of clay.

Turning jug forms can be awkward because the pinched lip often distorts the level of the rim. Accordingly a 'chum' or bed of clay can be

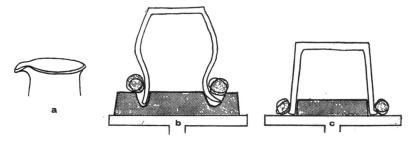

40. a) *Pinching lip of jug distorts level of rim;*
    b) *Clay chum for turning a jug;*
    c) *Use of chum on wheelhead with clay wads holding pot*

turned on the wheel head and a suitable groove cut away to accommodate the lip. A 'chum' is also useful in allowing a speedy removal of a pot for examination and a speedy replacement.

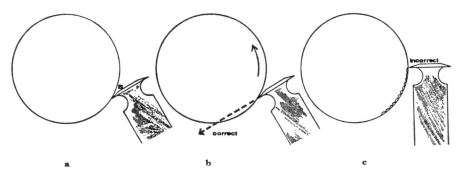

41. a) *Unless a good bevel is ground on tool point, it will foul pot; b) Fine shaving angle at 4 or 5 o'clock avoids chatter; c) Scraping angle at right angle to pot (at 3 o'clock) produces chattering*

To turn or shave away the surplus clay, two types of tools can easily be made. An eight inch long piece of $\frac{7}{8}$ in. by $\frac{1}{8}$ in. mild steel can be shaped with a file and the last 1 in. bent at right angles, or a looped wire tool can be made from 4 inches of 14 swg. wire and a 7 in. piece of $\frac{3}{8}$ in. dowel rod, or a handle from an old paint brush. The wire is beaten for $1\frac{1}{2}$ in. in the middle to $\frac{3}{16}$ in. in width, bent as in diagram and then bound with copper wire (a strand from a piece of electric cable) to the wood handle (figure 42).

31

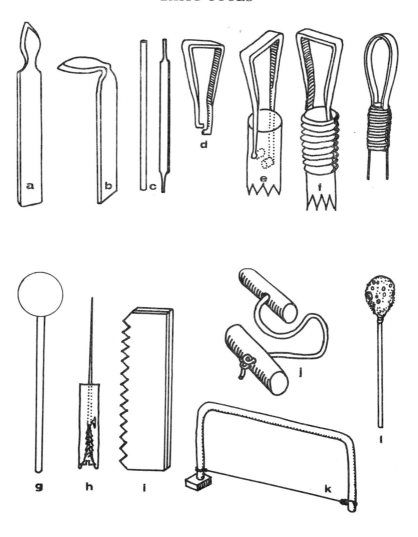

42. *a, b) Filed cutting bevel and then end is bent at 90° in vice; c, d) 14 s.w.g. wire hammered flat and then bent to shape; e, f) ⅜ in. dowel handles with two holes drilled to take wire ends, copper wire binding; g) Wood ball glued on end of ⅜ in. dowel for inside pots; h) Cycle spoke screwed home in end of dowel; i) Piece of hacksaw blade; j) ⅜ in. dowel handles with nylon (100 lb.) or wire for cutting off; k) ⅜ in. mild steel frame with piano wire threaded through one leg which is compressed against other end to make taut; l) Sponge wired onto stick*

Whichever tool is used, it is essential that by supporting the arms, it is held steadily against the pot at about the 4 o'clock position. Its cutting edge, which must be kept sharp, is best adjusted in relation to the pot to give an even and clean cut without 'chattering' or biting too deeply into the clay. Chattering occurs if the turning tool is not sharp or has insufficient bevel or is held at a scraping angle instead of a shaving angle.

If the base is at all irregular, it is advisable to start by making an incision with the firmly held point or edge of the tool allowing it to cut more or less into the circumference. In this way an accurate start is made which enables the turning process to be carried out successfully. Uneven turning will result if the tool is allowed to move with the eccentricity of the base. Knowing how much clay to remove to produce a uniform thickness of wall comes with experience. Some 'musical' potters claim to be able to tell the thickness by listening to the note made by tapping the wall of the pot. The 'leather hard' condition of the clay is of course important and if it is a 'soft leather hardness' then a controlled finger pressure on the wall of the pot at a couple of places will indicate, by a slightly lesser resistance, that the thickness is right; especially if the inside shape has been carefully assessed before inverting the pot onto the wheel.

There are many traditional styles for turning the foot of a pot but always the shape and character of the finished form must be taken into account (p. 50). Adequate stability must be a major requirement, but it is quite surprising just how narrow a foot can be to satisfy this need; and if a pot is considered as an 'object in space', then clearly the narrower the base, the more this feeling will be satisfied. The foot, like the rim, exerts a very great influence on the final product and can do much to produce a 'lift' or create a point from which the main form is able to spring or grow.

43. Turning the base

CHAPTER FIVE

SLABBED POTS

The making of pots out of slabs of clay might at first appear a little un-exciting yet the scope offered by this method is vast and not only opens up another field of exploration but can provide a valuable change even from throwing when, as in all human endeavours, a temporary staleness occurs. This technique has been called 'clay joinery', an appropriate term if it only serves to emphasize the great care that is needed in joining pieces together. For in each of the many ways in which pots can be built from slabs, three fundamental points must always be observed. First, the slab must be cut or rolled to a uniform thickness from a well prepared piece of clay. Second, it must be in the right condition of hardness to maintain its shape. Third, the joins must be most carefully made.

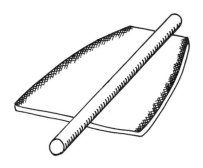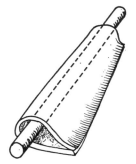

44. Shaped slab with a rolling pin   *45. Slab folded and edges firmly pressed together*

A simple slabbed pot can be made by folding over a sheet of clay and fixing it to a base. Cut a slab of clay to shape with a needle (fig. 44). Generously daub each long end for about half an inch in width with thick slip or slurry. Lay a round rod or thin rolling pin down the centre and fold the damp clay over to bring the two slipped surfaces into contact. Press them firmly together, raise the edge just off the bench and pinch it between the finger and thumb to produce a direct constructional pattern. Cut a slab of clay a little bigger than required for the base and allow it to dry out with the shape supported by the rod until almost leather hard. If necessary pieces can be kept in a damp cupboard for assembling and finishing later.

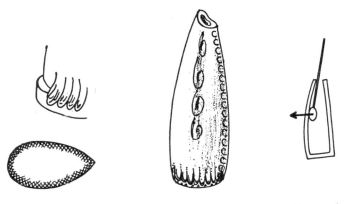

46. *Base cut out and joined onto base modelling upwards*   47. *Base modelled to body*   48. *Tool for coaxing out sagging walls*

Remove the rod and place the hollow form vertically onto the base which is then cut $\frac{1}{8}$ in. bigger all round. Remove the top, slip its bottom edge and the base, and firmly press it down onto the base. Model up the outside edge of the base into the wall of the pot. If the size of the neck allows, a thin coil of clay can be modelled into the inside seam with a long stick. If necessary, gently coax the inside of the walls outwards with a suitable tool such as a rod with a ball fixed at the end. The outside can be textured or patterned as desired.

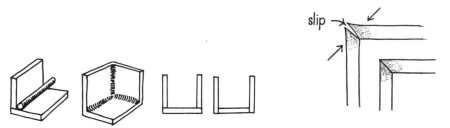

49. *Thin coil for seam; coils firmly modelled to inner surfaces; walls built on base (left) and not around it; finished corner with edges cut at just over 45°*

When making two, three or four sided pots the edges of the slabs are perhaps best cut at just over 45° to make the strongest join. They must be well slipped and where possible a thin coil should be modelled along the inside seams. Various possibilities for shapes, including the use of a top are indicated in figs. 50, 53, 80. Templates cut from thin card to a desired shape can be placed onto clay slabs, marked round and cut out with a needle. For curved walls the slabs, cut to shape, are best allowed to become leather hard by supporting them with wads of clay or placing them in

50. *a) Wads of clay supporting curved slab; b) Hammock for curved slab; c) single slab dish; d, e) pots from two slabs*

a scrim or mesh 'hammock' (fig. 50b). There is a tendency for the walls of 'flat' sided pots to become concave on drying out or firing and this hollowing often produces a weaker looking form. Accordingly it is good practice to make the walls very slightly convex when in the damp state. For just as the Greeks discovered the need of entasis for their columns to prevent the optical illusion of appearing waisted in the middle, so does a flat form require slight convexity to maintain its feeling of strength.

Another way of using slabs of clay is to press them into or over a mould. Thus one slab of clay can produce a dish shape while the joining of two or more moulded slabs can produce pot forms (fig. 50). Many objects to hand can be used as moulds and if their surface is too smooth to allow the clay to shrink away as it dries out, then it can be dusted with powdered clay or flint to reduce suction. Pottery, wood, or stainless steel plates and dishes, and papier maché or plastic trays used for pre-packing meat and fruit, can serve well. Two coal shovels can be used to make a flat bottle form attached to a suitable base. The making in plaster of simple one or two-piece moulds, however, is quite easy and enables a planned rather than a makeshift form to be made. Make a solid clay model on the wheel or on a board so that its base is uppermost. Smooth the surface with a sponge and preferably a kidney rubber before fixing a strip of lino around the form with wads of clay. The joins of the lino are 'clamped' with clothes pegs or a piece of string is tied around the outside. Next, judge the volume of the space to receive plaster and pour this approximate quantity of water into a bowl. Slowly sprinkle fine plaster of Paris into the water until a mound accumulates in the middle. Stir the mixture with the hand, squeezing out the more solid masses, until an even creamy consistency is obtained. Tap the bowl on the bench to bring any air to the surface and as soon as a finger drawn across the mixture leaves a 'track', pour the plaster over the form to cover it to about one inch above its base. As a guide, about 30 ounces of plaster are needed for one pint of water. When plaster begins to set an exothermic reaction takes place. As soon as the plaster feels warm remove the lino and turn the clay shape and plaster upside down. If carefully extracted, the clay can be used again, but under no circumstances should pots be made from clay that is contaminated with plaster as the sulphur in it (calcium sulphate) is liable to cause 'spitting out' in the glaze. For this reason the sharp edges on the mould are best scraped clean with a ruler.

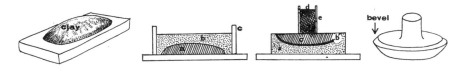

51. Making a press mould: clay model; plaster mould with lino walls; stout paper cylinder and second plaster; inverted hump mould with ¼ in. bevel

This hollow mould can now be used to make from it a hump mould. Either gently lather several coats of soft soap, or pour a very thin clay slip over the surface so that a fine film of soap or clay is formed. This will prevent the second pouring of plaster from adhering to the first. Prepare a suitably sized cylinder of cartridge paper fastened with tape or paper clips for the stand. Pour plaster into the mould and at the first sign of setting, place the paper cylinder in position and fill it with plaster. Hold the cylinder still until the plaster just sets. Carefully remove the paper, add plaster at the join between cylinder and mould and smooth off the new plaster flush with the old. Remove the hump from the hollow mould by pouring water onto it to soften the clay slip lining, and with a controlled rocking movement the two pieces will come apart. The edges will now require fettling with a knife or rasp to give a bevel at right angles to the line of the mould of from ¼ in. to ½ in. in width.

To make a dish from a hollow mould place it on a banding wheel, lay a slab of clay ¼ in. to ⅜ in. thick over the mould and gently coax it as far into the hollow as possible. With a needle inserted and maintained at 90°, cut off the obvious surplus clay. Support one part of the edge at a time and with a damp sponge gently dab and stroke the clay to make contact first at the base and then at the side of the mould. Re-trim the clay to within ¼ in. of the edge of the mould and firmly sponge the clay from the base upwards. Having ensured close contact between the clay and

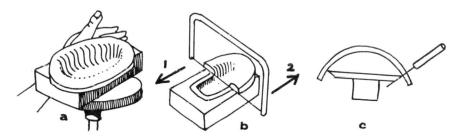

52. a) *Supporting edge of slab for hollow dish; b) 1st cut and 2nd cut made; c) Needle held on bevel while mould is rotated to trim edge of hump dish*

the edge of the mould, use a cutting frame to make flush the edges by drawing it from the centre towards the near side of the mould. Thus at least two such strokes will be required. As the clay dries, it shrinks away from the mould and sharp taps with the base of the hand on the edge of the mould's face will help this process. Place a board over the mould, carefully invert it and the board and lift up the mould to leave the dish to dry as required upside down on the board. The edge can be re-cut at 90° to the slope of the walls. A hollow moulded dish lends itself particularly to slipping or slip trailing as the mould itself supports the damp clay and facilitates the holding of the shape when pouring out surplus ground slip. Clean off any slip on the top of the mould so that in drying out, the form can shrink freely from the rim and so prevent possible splitting. When dry, hold the dish over a bowl of water and then with tow or glass paper, smooth the edges with long strokes, allowing the clay dust to settle in the water rather than in the lungs! If the dish when dry is *gently* turned around on an old kiln shelf, a very satisfactory finish is given to the edge of the dish. A final finish can be made with a damp sponge.

To make a hump moulded dish the mould can again be placed on a banding wheel. Carefully position the slab of clay over the mould, press it gently onto the base and immediately cut off the surplus edge to within a $\frac{1}{2}$ in. or so of the mould. Starting from the centre, dab the clay with a wet sponge all over the base and then the sides, followed by stroking movements spirally downwards. When contact with the edge of the mould is achieved, press a thin needle from the outside edge of the clay to rest on the bevel of the mould, and tilt it a little downwards so that as the mould is turned the firmly held needle cuts the clay tending to pull it towards the surface of the mould (fig. 52c). The arris can now be decorated by repeating thumb nail or tool impressions, or gently sponged clean. If a damp slice of clay is used, this method of making is particularly suitable for thin coiled-clay decoration. First damp the hump mould and then position very thin coils of perhaps red clay into an all over pattern. Press or beat them flat with a block of wood onto the surface of the mould. The damp slab of clay is then very carefully positioned over the mould so that when it is pressed on firmly the coiled pattern is readily merged into the clay to produce a low relief decoration.

53. *Narrow slabbed pot*

54. *Thin coiled decoration on surface of mould prior to placing damp slab of clay*

SLIP CASTING

Slip casting, much employed in industry, is a useful way of making deep dish shapes that are too awkward for pressing. Liquid clay is poured into the mould to just fill it. This level must be maintained by topping up as the plaster absorbs water. After a few minutes the mould is inverted and allowed to stand on two sticks, so that surplus slip can drain out and a coating of thicker slip completely covers the surface of the mould. When 'dull dry' the mould is set upright again and the edges trimmed with a needle. As soon as the slip-clay form shrinks from the mould it is best covered with a bat and inverted. The mould is then lifted off to allow the shape to dry out evenly in an upside down position. When dry, the edges are fettled with tow which can be concocted from 2 in. lengths of parcel string teased out to make a loose pad.

It is clear that the wetter the slip, the more water will have to be obsorbed to produce the desired thickness of wall. It is advisable, therefore, to use slip that has been specially prepared for casting. Depending on the type of clay body, about three pints of water when added to 12 lbs of powdered clay will give a very thick slip which is far too sluggish for casting. By first dissolving 20 cc. (about a dessert-spoonful) of sodium silicate in the three pints of hot water the resulting slip becomes very fluid after standing for twenty four hours, and suitable for the easy filling and emptying of moulds. Before use moulds should be dried out thoroughly, preferably in a low oven heat, or suitably supported on top of a warm kiln, so that they become absorbent.

CHAPTER SIX

COMPOSITE POTS

Pots with lids, handles, spouts or feet are composed of more than one part and different methods of making can be used to combine them into a harmonious whole. With lidded pots there are at least five distinct treatments to choose from (fig. 55). Each type has its own particular quality

55. Various types of lids

and greatly influences the character of the finished pot. Thus in **c** the treatment of the rim of the lid plays the same important role as the lip of the body **b** so that in the final statement of the form the lid of **c** assumes a much greater importance than the lid of **b**. Of course, the use of the pot may well dictate the type of lid required so that a tea pot demands a deep flanged lid to prevent its falling out when the pot is tilted for pouring. Tradition too tends to associate for example **a** with butter dishes or jam pots, **b**, or **c** with casseroles, **d** with storage jars, **e** with tobacco jars and **f** with powder bowls. This wealth of choice, together with the need for considering the proportion and style of an appropriate knob, makes lidded pots a particularly fascinating study, and it can be attempted at an early stage in 'accurate' coiling, by making a marmalade pot or butter dish. Two accurate coils are modelled onto a 3 in. or 4 in. diameter base, and after pleating are thrown up from the base to give walls of about ¼ in. thickness. Having trimmed the rim, a seating is made by pressing a finger from the outside towards the inside followed by a ruler end held as in figure 56. For the lid a slice of clay less than ¼ in. thick is cut out and placed over a domed plaster bat that has been made to fit into an extractor wheel head (fig. 57). Calipers are adjusted to the diameter. The clay is sponged onto the revolving bat and the edge trimmed with a needle. The diameter is checked with the calipers so that a second cut should produce the correct size. A small piece of clay, the size of a walnut, is modelled firmly on the centre and carefully 'thrown' to shape. When

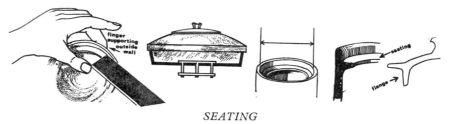

SEATING

56. *Thumb sup-porting ruler held in right hand*

57. *Domed shaped mould in extractor wheel cup*

58. *Seating measurement*

59. *Seating and its flange*

sufficiently dry the lid can be tapped from the bat and placed into the seating of the leather-hard pot the base of which has been previously turned. Thus this early exercise will give practice in some aspects of coiling, throwing and slabbing.

60. Various types of knobs

Handles can be made by coiling, wire-cutting, press moulding or pulling. The size and style of the handle must be in keeping with the pot and it is worth noting just how small the handle need be to produce a happy balance. Coils used as handles tend to be clumsy; wire-cut handles, made by pulling a piece of looped wire through a thick coil of clay have a certain formality about them which can make them suitable for more

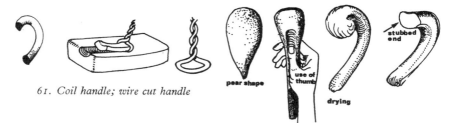

61. Coil handle; wire cut handle

62. Stages in making a 'pulled' handle

precise forms; handles pressed out in a two-piece mould are suitable for industrial ware; but pulled handles are usually appropriate for all types of

42

pots since they have a certain vitality of their own. They are made by grasping a pear shaped piece of well prepared clay in the left hand while the wetted right hand coaxes the mass downwards to form a tail. A flatter rather than rounder section is usually more lively and a certain amount of tapering is acceptable. The tip of the right thumb squeezed against the fingers and down the middle of the handle can help in producing the desired section. When pulled, the mass of clay is pressed firmly onto a board to allow the handle to assume a naturally curved shape. When almost leather hard, it is cut off clean with a knife and stubbed with the thumb or finger nail to increase the thickness of clay that is needed where it joins the pot. The leather hard pot is slipped at the points of attachment and the stubbed end of the handle is pressed firmly against

63. End well stubbed for cup or jug handle; horizontal handle; lug handles from half cylinders

the top point, supported by a finger opposite on the inside. Care must be taken to sight across the diameter of the rim to see that the handle is correctly aligned. The top is then carefully modelled on, the required curve of the handle adjusted and the bottom pressed onto the slipped lower spot on the pot. Three direct movements of the finger or thumb are sufficient to join the handle securely at its bottom end to the pot, but if hygiene is of importance, a very thin roll of clay can be modelled on the inside of the join. A successfully pulled handle, growing out of the pot and back into it again, does in fact give the feeling of being an integral part of the finished form and not something 'just stuck on'. The handle may set to a better curve if the pot is allowed to dry upside down. While most pots have handles which are applied vertically, the same kind of pulled handle can be fixed horizontally to the casserole type of pot. Thrown narrow cylinders or their carefully cut sections can also be used to great advantage (fig. 63).

Lips for jugs can be made either immediately after throwing, by pulling the rim outwards against supporting fingers, or by gently beating with a round stick when the clay is nearly leather hard (fig. 64). Pots that require spouts are perhaps the most difficult of all to make successfully. Much consideration is necessary to make the various parts in the right proportion, and their positioning and joining together calls for a fine sense of balance.

65. *Thrown waisted spout showing cuts for lip and body*

66. *Balancing handle with spout*

64. *'pulled' or beaten lip*

Tea pot spouts are thrown as small conical forms, and when leather hard are cut at an angle to produce a good pouring lip. The sharper this lip, the more likely will it 'cut off the last drop of tea'. Stroking the last inch of the inside will also ensure a better flow. The base of the spout is marked all round and by trial and error, cut and trimmed to fit the body. Its contour is marked onto the body and with a reversed pen-knib as many holes as possible are 'drilled' within the marked area. Before applying the spout with slip, it is important to see that these holes are clean on both sides to prevent accumulation of tea leaves. For good pouring, the total area of the holes should be five times that of the narrowest sectional area of the spout. For this reason it can be a practical advantage to 'waist' slightly the spout towards the top. The top of the spout must, of course, not be below the body opening.

Like other composite parts of a pot, a foot or feet can take various forms and are equally dramatic in their effect on the form which is immediately

67-68. *Shallow bowls raised on 3 'pulled' feet*

69. *Bowl inverted to show 3 feet from thrown cones*

44

given a 'lift' or a feeling of being an object in space. Almost any shallow dish can be raised effectively by the addition of three pulled or cut triangular shaped feet which must be carefully positioned to produce a balance. Thrown cones of clay can be added in the same way to bowls of perhaps a greater depth or to very large free-formed coiled pots. Such pots can be started by pressing a slab of clay into a suitably shaped mould before continuing its form with coils. The supporting plaster mould enables the walls to be built at once and if some form of foot is to be added later, then quite dramatic shaped moulds can be used to produce pots of sculp-

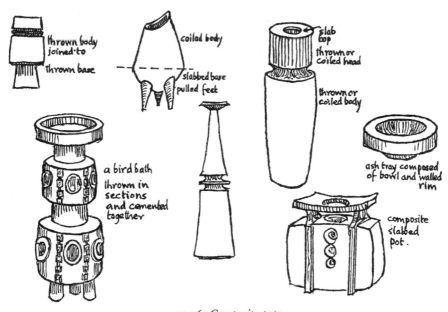

70-76. Composite pots

tural qualities. A single foot of the same shape as the body, whether square or round, but smaller in size, can often be added with effect and a coiled or thrown cylinder of the right proportion can be used to 'lift' almost any shaped pot. In this way, two forms are combined to produce the whole. It follows, that from a reasonably early stage, it is possible by such assembly of units to make pots of considerable size. All techniques of making or combinations of methods can be used to produce such results providing that great care is taken in modelling the sections together. It is important

45

that sections to be joined are in the same state of dampness, otherwise they will split apart on drying out or firing. The drying out must proceed very slowly indeed.

This composite method with its sculptural quality is particularly suitable for outside work such as sun-dials and bird baths; the various sections can later be cemented together with one part fine sand to one part of cement, or with Araldite. In this way, even a very small kiln can be used to produce work of considerable power and size (figs. 70-76).

CHAPTER SEVEN

DESIGN AND DECORATION

As soon as the craftsman has gained a measure of competence in the various skills discussed, he is at once involved in aesthetic considerations. Such terms as form, proportion, balance, movement, pattern, colour and texture are elements common to every art form. The spontaneity of pottery making and the intimate working nature of clay perhaps make for a much more immediate insight into an understanding of these basic elements of art than in any other medium. Pottery is personal, and the naming of the very parts of a 'typical pot' imply at once its living qualities – the lip, mouth, neck, shoulder, belly, waist, body and foot. Art has to do with life; it is a communication of a feeling for, or a comment on some aspect of life. The qualities of strength, calm, elegance, power, generosity, re-straint, gaiety - these are the feelings that are expressed to make a state-ment, to create a tension, to give vitality and meaning to the finished form. The basis of a satisfying piece of work must lie essentially in its form or structure or design. It is the function of decoration to emphasize or enrich the basic requirements of form by texture, pattern, and colour, always taking into account the basic form.

Demonstrate to twenty individuals the making of a simple cylinder shaped pot, and the twenty pots made in response will be as different as the facial variations of the individual makers. The slightest touch to the rim, making it a little thicker or thinner, sloping it slightly inwards or outwards, or holding it horizontal; keeping its outside vertical or allowing it to flare a suspicion outwards – such subtleties are at once readily apparent and they are the aesthetic choices that have to be made at every stage of progression. Involvement in such choices at once provokes the excite-ment and interest that enables the potter to express something of himself in his work. The creative urge is able to find meaningful expression and in some little measure 'art is born'. As technical skill improves, so too do the opportunities increase in scope; such is the perpetual struggle in the arts.

It might be helpful to consider some of the effects of construction, proportion, balance and movement on form by reference to the accompanying diagrammatic sketches. A pot thrown on the wheel is capable of a spontaneity that can be achieved in no other way. The throwing marks, spiralling to the top of such a pot, are of the essence of the method of construction and can well add to the rhythm of the final form (fig. 77). Coiling on a wheel is a slower process allowing of more deliberation and tends to produce a more studied form (fig. 78). A coiled pot made on a bench permits of non-circular base plans (fig. 79), and it is particularly suitable for textured surfacing. Slab built pots permit of flat sides and have forms in keeping with their 'clay joinery' method of construction (fig. 80).

77. Thrown pot; 78. Coiled on wheel; 79. Coiled on bench; 80. Slabbed pot

By increasing the proportion of the height to the width, a strong cylinder becomes more elegant (fig. 81). Vary the proportions of the base to the mouth and a greater sense of 'growth' is produced (fig. 82). Balance is concerned with the happy relationship of the several proportions that make up the form. Thus variations in the horizontal interval of division of a cylinder and in the width of the base will alter considerably the balance of the form (figs. 83, 84). If the width of one of the sections of each pot is changed, a much more complicated choice is offered (figs. 85, 86). This is

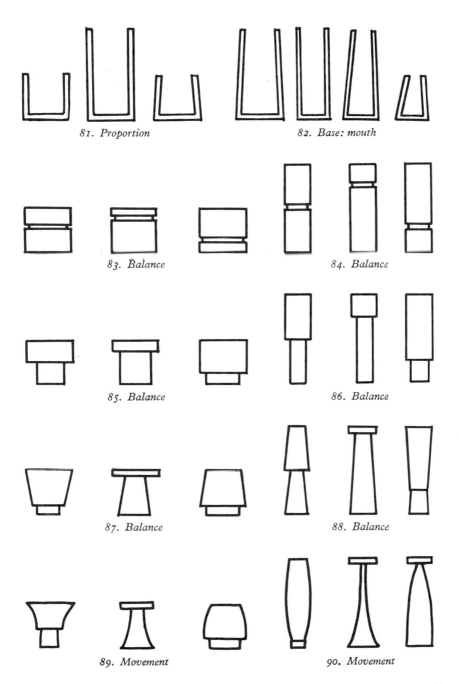

81. *Proportion*

82. *Base: mouth*

83. *Balance*

84. *Balance*

85. *Balance*

86. *Balance*

87. *Balance*

88. *Balance*

89. *Movement*

90. *Movement*

49

further increased by varying the widths of the top and the bottom of one or both sections (figs. 87, 88) and by the introduction of curved walls which also affect the movement (figs. 89, 90).

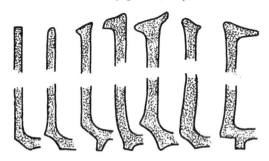

91. Lip and foot treatments influence character of final form

To such varied basic forms the treatment of the foot, and especially the lip, will do much to emphasize the character of the final form (fig. 91). These can be compared with the introduction and conclusion of an essay.

Of course, an experienced potter is able to conceive what his finished work will look like even before he chooses his clay. He will know that he intends to produce a powerful form to exploit the texture of a coarsely grogged clay with a proportion of oxide perhaps to develop the desired colour in a reduced or oxidised stoneware kiln, or that a fine plastic clay will best produce an elegant earthenware teapot. Only the details of decoration remain to be worked out from a preconceived consideration of the final product.

CONSIDERATIONS ON DECORATION

Many pots may well be best decorated by a suitable glaze, but the desire to embellish is innate to the human race and the sympathetic quality of clay and glaze provide the opportunity to satisfy this urge. Perhaps the prime justification for decorating pottery however is to exploit the exciting possibilities that the ceramic materials allow. Having arrived at an acceptable form, it is useful to look at it from a distance and then to move forward and touch the form where the eye has been drawn. This is the focal area of the pot where the eye wants naturally to rest, before, and after moving around to take in what the form has to say. It can often help therefore to consider this area carefully so that any decoration may act as a foil or an emphasis of its importance (figs. 92, 93). Decoration for fig. 93, might

50

consist of glazing the top half and leaving the lower half unglazed. The division would then take into account the full swelling of the body and

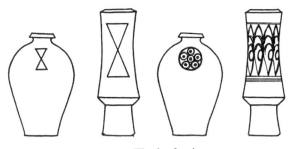

92-95. The focal points

shoulder which requires emphasis, while the lower section remains subordinate. In this case a stoneware body with an ash glaze might be appropriate. Added interest could be achieved by scratching a pattern into the clay so that the depth of glaze in the incisions will provide subtle colour variations. Such an expansive shoulder area might also invite a medallion type decoration in the form of sprigging (fig. 94). The form in fig. 93 suggests division by bands where the strongest motif is positioned around the focal point (fig. 95).

Banding, either by simple lines or developed motifs is a peculiarly suitable method of decoration for a circular pot.

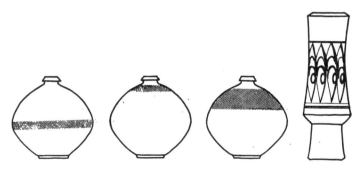

96. Position of bands :
Too low; too high; correct; too low

Consideration must be given to its position and width in relation to the other sections so formed (fig. 96). The method selected for decoration is largely dependent on the type of clay and style of pot.

51

Slip trailing is particularly suitable for open bowls and dishes. Slip is a sieved, creamy mixture of clay and water to which metal oxides as colourants can be added. A ground slip is applied to a bowl by partially filling it with slip and while it is being emptied, rotating it between the hands, finishing by holding the bowl in an inverted position for the slip to drain off. Slip for this purpose must not be too thick – a test is to use a

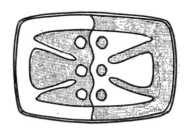

97. Slip trailing

large brush for stirring the slip and to check that when the brush is removed, the slip will flow from the brush in a slow steady stream. Another coloured slip is then filled into a trailer which is held close to the ground slip and a pattern is freely 'drawn'. The pot is then gently tapped on the bench to enable the trailed slip to bed into the still wet ground slip. More interesting results can be achieved by ground slipping in two colours and trailing each section with the opposite colour as in figure 97.

98. Fine sgraffito

99. Bold sgraffito

Slip sgraffito consists in applying a coloured ground slip to a smooth clay and then scratching a pattern through to the body. Bold treatment is best if the clay is damp but if a thin ground slip is allowed to become leather hard, very fine detail can be obtained (figs. 98, 99).

Carving and texturing are methods particularly appropriate for bolder hand built pots. A coarse toothed blade as used in the making of the pot, can produce interesting surfaces by itself. All-over patterns can be made by

100. Carving and texturing

impressing the clay with any suitably shaped implement to hand, the repetition of the shape making the pattern. Carving enables a vigorous pattern to be made but at first it may be best employed to create an all-over texture or an all-over repeating pattern, care being taken to balance the different proportions in relation to the general form (fig. 100). In earthenware the finish might consist of brushing a mixture of oxides over the surface and then tin-glazing, or of rubbing powdered metals into the clay or biscuit and glazing only the inside of the pot.

Sprigging is a comparatively little used method in studio pottery yet is capable of most interesting results. It consists of applying thin clay motifs to the clay form. A simple shape of suitable size is drawn on a flat piece of plaster and cut out about ⅛ in. in depth. A pattern is then tooled into

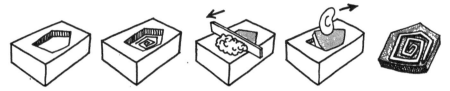

101. Sprigging: Motif marked on plaster and cut ⅛ in. deep; pattern carved in sunken area; clay pressed in and rulered off; sprigging removed with a clay wad; finished sprig

the sunken area. Damp clay is pressed in and firmly smoothed off level. A small wad of clay is then dabbed onto the surface to adhere just sufficiently to allow the sprigged motif to be removed from the mould and then from the clay wad. The sprigging and the pot are then slipped and the motif is pressed carefully but firmly onto the pot. This method allows the use of coloured clays, of single medallion treatment or of repeating motifs around a form (figs. 103, 104). A less formal method of clay application is to slip and press onto the surface small wads or thin coils of clay

102-104. Informal sprigging; single motif; repeating motifs

which can then be shaped and textured individually (fig. 102). This method permits of 'trial and error' decoration and so invites study and experiment in appropriateness to form. It is particularly suitable in stoneware with dolomite, ash, or 10% iron glazes where qualities of restraint act as a foil to the boldness of this technique.

DECORATION IN THE BISCUIT STATE

Metal oxides can be applied directly onto the biscuit and then glazed, or brushed on top of the raw powdered glaze, or both.

Free brush stroke painting is perhaps the most difficult form of decoration. To be successful, it requires a sure hand and an intuitive or practised sense of 'rightness' in relation to form. It is best approached by painting strokes within carefully chosen bands or as a built up all-over pattern. It is advisable at first to use the oxides in weaker rather than stronger mixtures, and the addition of some gum tragacanth will result in a smoother application to the biscuit with less tendency to 'bleed' into the glaze and will be less likely to be smudged when painted onto the raw glaze. Both underglaze and onglaze painting permit of no second chance unless glaze and

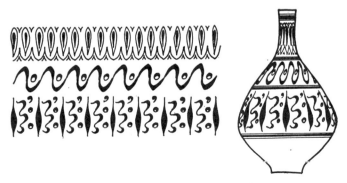

105. Free brushwork within bands

decoration are washed off and a new start made. This, together with the more stark and forbidding appearance that the biscuit form presents, makes the inevitable question 'where do I start?' even more pertinent (fig. 105).

Glaze sgraffito is fortunately a much more inviting technique and one which is essentially ceramic. Place the biscuit form on a banding wheel, charge a

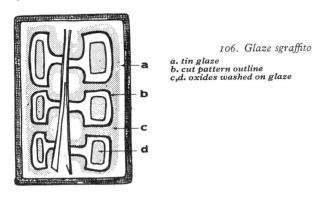

106. Glaze sgraffito
a. tin glaze
b. cut pattern outline
c,d. oxides washed on glaze

mop brush with thin pigment and hold it against the surface while slowly rotating the wheel. Cover the entire surface to within $\frac{1}{2}$ in. of the foot. Tin glaze the pot. Where the eye rests naturally, scratch through the glaze,

55

with a round pointed stick, a suitable shape and repeat this at intervals round the form. Connect these shapes and extend them where desired to produce an all-over pattern. The effect of the metal under a tin glaze, according to its thickness, will tint the whiteness of the tin and where the glaze has been removed will be a black line with a sheen. A more colourful product can be made by applying thin washes of oxides to areas as required and if necessary emphasising movement with full onglaze brush strokes. (fig. 106).

Onglaze sgraffito is a form of decoration that is in some ways similar to enamel groundlaying (page 86). A pot, having been tin-glazed and fired is either sprayed or brushed all over with a mixture of sieved metal oxide and a little gum tragacanth. In order to minimise the unevenness of application that a brush must inevitably give, a 1 in. camel hair varnish brush should be used. As soon as the pigment has dried, it can be scratched effectively with a wooden point. Areas can be wiped clean if required and quite fine texturing can be achieved. The ware is then fired a third time to glost temperature, and the pattern establishes itself firmly into the molten glaze. In this way it is much more permanent than enamel groundlaying which melts only into the surface of the glaze.

Cut paper shapes can assist greatly in producing bold results and are particularly suitable for open dishes. Wash the biscuit with a mixture of oxides and then tinglaze. Cut or tear a piece of thin paper (newsprint will

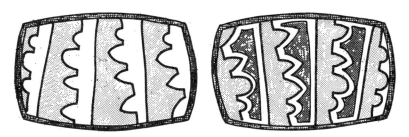

107. Cut paper alone   *108. Cut paper and glaze sgraffito*

do), damp it and by trial and error, select a suitable position on the form. Paint over the pot and paper pattern taking care not to pick up too much glaze. Remove the paper carefully and re-position and repeat if desired. If the result is unsatisfactory or if it has smudged, it may be corrected either by painting on another colour or by scratching through the glaze, or a combination of both (figs. 107, 108).

Stoneware decoration. Because of subtleties of colour and texture of clays glazes when fired to stoneware temperatures, the approach to this type of pottery demands decoration that exploits the exciting qualities that a 'natural' use of materials and firing give. Since a stoneware body is impervious to water, any selected part of a pot may be left unglazed so that the high fired body can be used effectively to contrast in colour and surface with the glaze. Because stoneware glazes are viscous in firing, a much greater depth of quality results. Such rocks as felspar and dolomite can be used in sufficient quantity in stoneware glazes to melt to a viscous state and so produce their granite-like or marble like qualities. Ash, containing its own metallic colourants in 'natural' proportion, produces waxy glazes, which according to the atmosphere of the kiln, give colours of the greatest interest (fig. 69).

Exhibitions and museums. It is of very great value to see both modern and traditional work at exhibitions and museums if a fuller appreciation and understanding of one's own efforts is to be developed. Many local museums have good collections of past work, and in London the Victoria and Albert Museum and the British Museum are immensely rich in examples. Both the Crafts Centre, Earlham Street, London, W.2, and the Craftsmens' Potters' Association in Marshall Street (near Carnaby Street), London, W.1, with their changing displays are of particular interest in reflecting some of the modern developments. In addition, exhibitions of an individual or a group of potters are specially valuable because a collection of work gives a fuller insight into the mood and ideas and the style of the artist. It is hoped that the inclusion of some classical works of the past, alongside equivalent works of today, in the plates at the back of the present book will be helpful in indicating a standard worthy of appreciation and emulation (figs. 120 ff.).

CHAPTER EIGHT

GLAZE, GLAZING AND COLOURS

In many cases a clay form that has been made into pottery by firing, is complete by itself and needs no further treatment. A pottery flower pot and a milk or butter cooler, rely on their porous nature to perform their required functions, and unglazed vitreous stoneware forms which are watertight may well be satisfying as they are. If however, we require a porous body to be made watertight, if it is important to increase a pot's mechanical strength, if perhaps for hygienic reasons it is desirable to achieve a finer finish, and if, aesthetically a more pleasing result can be obtained, then covering all or part of its surface with a skin of glass will answer these needs. For glaze is essentially a glass, and silica is the ideal glass. Sand, flint and quartz are practically pure silica and if heated to about 1800° C. would in fact melt and form shiny glass on cooling. However, such a high temperature is impracticable and in any case would cause most ceramic bodies themselves to melt. It is necessary therefore to add something to the silica which will cause it to melt or flow or flux at a much lower temperature. Such a material is called a flux and the most amenable and powerful of all ceramic fluxes is lead. If one part of sand and three parts of powdered lead (red lead oxide) are mixed in an unglazed dish and made red hot, say 1000° C., then on cooling, the lead will have caused the silica (sand) to melt into a mass of shiny glass. In other words, the lead will have reacted with the silica to form lead silicate, or as every schoolboy knows, acid (silica) + base (lead) = salt (lead silicate). Of course this chemical reaction will only take place at a heat when the glass is in fact molten and it is in this condition that the ingredients of a glaze and other factors affecting it are able to play their part. Accordingly, we can best regard glaze as a super cooled liquid: like tar on the road, it is only on cooling that this liquid becomes solid. But as salts in the chemistry laboratory especially on slow cooling, tend to crystallise out, so too would a simple mixture of lead and sand produce a glass that would not be stable enough for use.

Some other base, or flux, therefore, such as soda ash, potash, borax or lime must replace some of the lead to produce at molten heat, more than one

58

chemical compound in solution which together will render the resulting glaze much more durable. In this connection, the durability of a glass or glaze is very considerably increased by the addition of even a small amount of alumina (from clay) which also helps to prevent crystallisation, or devitrification and gives strength to the glass. From this it can be seen that a satisfactory glaze must be made up from three types of material, the base (preferably more than one flux), the acid (silica) and alumina which is known as the intermediate or amphoteric. Since glazes may be fired at from about 1000° C. to 1400° C., it follows, especially if one considers the various raw materials from which these ingredients can be obtained, that the number of possible glaze recipes is in fact countless.

Ceramic chemists however have determined that according to the relative proportions of these three parts of a glaze the basic, the intermediate and the acidic, so will depend the temperature required for their fusion. If the proportion of the basic oxides is taken as 1 and denoted by RO, then glaze compositions of from:

$$\textbf{RO} - \textbf{1.5SiO}_2 \qquad \text{to} \qquad \textbf{RO} - \textbf{3SiO}_2$$

(1 part base to 1½ parts silica)　　(1 part base to 3 parts silica)

would give low firing glazes, while glazes from:

$$\textbf{RO} - \textbf{.1Al}_2\textbf{O}_3 - \textbf{2SiO}_2 \quad \text{to} \quad \textbf{RO} - \textbf{.9Al}_2\textbf{O}_3 - \textbf{5SiO}_2$$

(1 part base to $\frac{1}{10}$ part alumina to　(1 part base to $\frac{9}{10}$ part alumina to
　2 parts silica)　　　　　　　　　　5 parts silica)

would require much higher temperatures for fusion. From these formulae several very important practical facts emerge for the potter.

1). A glaze without alumina ($\textbf{RO-3SiO}_2$) melts at a lower temperature than a glaze containing less silica and only a little alumina ($\textbf{RO-.1Al}_2\textbf{O}_3- \textbf{2SiO}_2$).

2). The higher the proportion of alumina, the higher the point of fusion.

3). The higher the proportion of silica, the higher the point of fusion.

4). The proportion of alumina to silica should not exceed $\frac{1}{5}$.

Thus silica, regarded as an acid, is the core of a glaze and requires a material, a base, to make it flux at a lower temperature. More than one base is desirable to prevent a simple solid solution from tending to disintegrate by crystallisation or devitrification, and alumina is necessary to increase the durability and toughness of a glaze.

Glass is essentially silica and flux, whereas glaze is silica, flux and clay which stiffens the glass. Furthermore the addition of flint (glass) to a clay body, and clay to a glaze (glass), establishes a compatibility which tends to overcome the problems of expansion and contraction. Such an understanding of the fundamental character of a glaze should enable the potter to gain some insight into his materials and so to use them with perhaps a little more success.

Materials used in glazing are all natural earths, rocks or metals, and are thought of by the potter in terms of the part they play in a glaze. It is interesting to note some principal differences between glass making and ceramics to appreciate more fully the requirements of glaze materials. Molten glass is hardened by cooling while soft clay is hardened by firing. The glass maker's molten material can be thoroughly fluid in its furnace and is accessible for the skimming off of impurities. This fluidity means that coarser raw materials can be used, that air bubbles therefore will more readily escape and that a more intimate mix can be achieved. The method of glazing a ceramic body does not permit of these advantages. A glaze that is too fluid will run off the pot so that its fusing or maturing temperature must be within much finer limits than required for glass. This necessary lack of fluidity, its viscosity, tends towards the incomplete escapement of air bubbles which can remain imprisoned in the glaze. This, together with the comparative thinness of a glaze, demands that the materials be very finely ground, in fact waterground, to ensure the necessary chemical action for a good glaze. Furthermore, the glazing process does not permit removing any impurities or scum so that the materials must be especially pure. Thus while sand is commonly used in glass manufacture, the *acid* constituent, silica, for glazes, is obtained from the more pure flint or quartz. Cornish stone and felspar, considered later, can also be used. The *intermediate constituent* is always alumina, or alumina and borax. The alumina is obtained from clay (see page 12 flow chart), and although all clays will provide alumina, and perhaps other unwanted materials too, china clay and ball clay are generally used because of their purity. Again, to a lesser extent, felspar and cornish stone can be used. The *basic constituent* can be obtained from lead oxide, potash, soda ash, borax*, lime and felspar. Lead oxide, in the form of red lead, white lead or galena has been popular for centuries because of its readiness to combine with varying proportions of other glaze materials. In these raw states it is poisonous. Sodium compounds, used mainly in glass making, and potassium compounds almost invariably used for ceramic glazes, are both soluble in water. So too is borax but this is present in colemanite which is sufficiently

---

* Borax, because it can lower the melting point of a glaze, is here considered as a base, but because it can replace silica, it could be regarded as an acid. It also serves similarly to alumina in tending to prevent disintegration or devitrification and it is now generally included with alumina as an intermediate constituent. Perhaps such a problem at least serves to give some little insight to the layman of the vast complexities that confront the ceramic chemist.

insoluble for it to be used in its raw state. *Lime*, almost insoluble and usually in the form of whiting, is particularly useful in high temperature glazes.

The principle of glazing a porous biscuit pot demands that the ingredients be relatively insoluble in water. As the body absorbs the water from the glaze mixture to suck on the coating of powdered glaze, some of the soluble materials would otherwise continue with the water and so separate themselves from the glaze.

Accordingly soluble materials are made into *frits*. This consists of heating the soluble potash or borax with flint in a crucible, pouring the 'melt' so formed into cold water to shatter it and then grinding this 'soft' glass into a finely powdered 'frit'. For economy of firing, the frit is melted at a low temperature, finely ground and then as an insoluble powder, is incorporated with 'mill additions' such as clay and silica, to produce a durable glaze. By fritting lead its poisonous nature is overcome and it is transformed into a silicate. Clay is never fritted with flux because not only would it increase the melting temperature but its addition in a glaze recipe, because of extreme fineness helps to maintain the suspension of glaze ingredients when mixed with water. *Felspar*, mentioned above has been aptly described as 'nature's own frit', and is of special interest in stoneware glazes. Because it is composed of 17% potash, 18% alumina and 65% silica which appear to be reasonable proportions of the three basic requirements for a glaze, we should expect it to form a glaze by itself. In fact, at about 1300° C. felspar does melt to form a cloudy glass. The type of base or flux used largely determines the quality of the ceramic ware so that the chief basic constituent in a glaze, appropriately describes its family - thus a lead, an alkaline or a felspathic glaze.

CERAMIC COLOURS

Colours in pottery bodies and glazes are obtained from metal oxides, because they do not burn away on firing. If iron is left out in the weather it will go rusty. Oxygen from air, or water in the air, attacks the surface of the iron and combines with it to form a compound of iron and oxygen, iron or ferric oxide, which is rust red in colour. In fact, three parts of oxygen will readily join with two parts of iron to give Fe_2O_3. But iron and and oxygen will combine in various proportions and the oxides so formed may vary considerably in colour. Thus iron oxide, ferrous oxide, $Fe\ O$ has 28.5% oxygen and gives greens, while ferrosic oxide, Fe_3O_4 has 38% oxygen and gives black or purplish black. The shiny black crust on a forged horseshoe is ferrosic oxide and known as 'blacksmith's scale' or 'spangles'. Rust can easily be ground into a fine powder and can therefore be made into a smooth pigment which will disperse evenly throughout a glaze or clay slip. Metals therefore are prepared by potter's merchants in their oxide forms and are finely ground for use as ceramic colourants. Most metals, when dissolved in a glaze will give colour. Some examples are shown in the table below:

metal oxide	oxidation colour	reduction colour
Iron	Amber rust brown black	Olive green (celadon) purple black
Copper	bright green in lead glaze green turquoise in alkaline black if thick	red purple (flambé)
Cobalt	blue	blue
Manganese	purplish brown	purplish brown
Chromium	green (with tin—pink but its volatile nature can cause unwanted 'blushing' on other ware)	green
Nickel	green-grey	green-grey
Uranium ⎫ Vanadium ⎬ very expensive Selenium ⎭	red and yellow yellow (with tin) red and yellow	

Many factors can affect the colour obtained.

Remembering that it is when the glaze is a molten liquid that chemical changes occur, it is clear that the amount of metal in relation to the thickness (the amount) of glaze is of particular importance. If too much oxide is applied to a pot then there will be insufficient liquid glass to dissolve it completely. Accordingly a black metallic area will occur.

If not excessive, copper can be effectively used this way since where the metal is a little thinner it 'bleeds' into the surrounding glaze to produce a characteristic bright green and so add particular interest in an opaque glaze. However, if the amount of metal is excessive, then black copper oxide in an unpleasant dry and rough form will occur. Other colours can be made by mixing metals together although to apply one metal over another will not give the top colour as with oil paints, but a combination of both, because they will both dissolve and play their parts in the liquid glaze. While the metals sodium (in soda ash), potassium (in potash), and lead do not give colour, yet in correct proportions they can have an influence on other metals. Thus copper will give a bluish green in a strongly acidic glaze and a yellower green in a basic glaze. The 'atmosphere' of the kiln too can have a dramatic effect on colour so that iron will change from amber, and copper from green, in an oxidising atmosphere, to celadon green and red respectively in a reducing atmosphere (p. 69).

High temperature glazes, being particularly viscous or sluggish when molten, especially if thick, will result in incomplete fusion of all the glaze ingredients and the imprisonment of minute bubbles in the glaze matrix. Both will not only 'soften' the colour, but the air bubbles will cause a scattering of light to produce a depth and waxy quality that can be one of the delights peculiar to stoneware glazes. Particularly with such glazes it is well to remember that they consist of several distinct layers made up of surface materials from the body fluxing with adjacent glaze while the changing atmosphere of the kiln, allowing a greater or lesser penetration of oxidation, plays its part in affecting the colours of the different glaze layers. Thus the surface layer of a reduced glaze, or body is almost always oxidised as air enters the kiln on cooling. This accounts for the warm red rust of an unglazed stoneware body which if broken would reveal a grey colour.

As indicated above, metals are used in the form of powdered oxides. It is not the colour of the oxide that is important but rather the colour it will give when dissolved in a particular type of glaze fired to a certain temperature in an oxidising or reducing kiln atmosphere. Oxides of cobalt, copper, manganese and iron can be black but they produce their own specific colour in the molten glaze solution. It is essential therefore that jars of metal oxides be clearly labelled and that the contents be kept uncontaminated. Again, green copper carbonate, red copper oxide or black copper oxide will each give the same colour in the glaze matrix. So also will red iron oxide, black iron oxide or yellow iron oxide. There are, however, reasons why one form of metal oxide might be preferable to another. First, if the four common metals are considered they could be distinguished more easily if *red* iron oxide, *green* copper carbonate, *black* manganese oxide, and *grey* (nearly black) cobalt oxide were used. But of more importance is the comparative size of particle. For example, grey cobalt is finer than black cobalt so that because of the extremely powerful colour strength of this metal, the larger particle is more likely to produce small concentrations to give deep blue specks in the finished glaze, while copper carbonate being less dense and weaker in colour strength than black copper oxide will not paint onto a body so easily but also will tend not to produce metallic areas quite so readily. In the same way, black iron oxide is inclined to break through a stoneware glaze to give large black specks more easily than the red or scarlet iron oxide.

TYPES OF GLAZES

Glazes can be considered from various points of view, e.g. raw glazes made from insoluble materials, and lead, leadless, alkaline, boracic or felspathic glazes. They can also be classified as follows according to the kind of finish they give.

Transparent glazes give a shiny finish and are particularly suitable for coloured slipware and colours used under the glazes on a smooth ivory or white body.

Coloured transparent glazes. These are made by the addition of suitable metal oxides. Since metals cause the glaze to flow more freely, such glazes require a lower firing temperature if they are not to run and stick to the kiln shelf. Alternatively, a little china clay can be added to counter this running or the amount of basic element can be reduced.

Matt glazes are made by adding zinc, or titanium (rutile) to earthenware glazes which produce minute crystallisation on cooling. China clay is preferable for stoneware glazes.

Opaque glazes are made by adding to a transparent glaze about 10% of tin oxide which produces a dense white glaze. Such glazes were used to impart to clays a smooth surface which was freely painted upon by the Persians and Turks. This tin-glazed ware was made successively in various parts of Europe. The best known types are the Hispano-Moresque, Majolica, Faience, Delft, and Lambeth tin-glazed pottery. A cheaper metal, zirconium behaves similarly to tin but produces a less 'fat' surface. It can be used very successfully with tin to produce interesting variations in surface texture and quality.

Salt glazes are unique and are made by introducing common salt into the kiln atmosphere at about 1200° C. At this temperature the salt vaporises and produces hydrochloric acid and soda. The soda reacts with the silica, alumina, lime and iron in the ceramic body to produce a durable and perfect fitting glaze. Sewer pipes, which are made from iron-bearing clay, are the commonest form of this ware and both the browns of English oxidised fired ware and the purplish blacks of continental reduced fired ware have a distinctive orange peel texture of their own. It is evident that not only the separately standing ware becomes glazed, but eventually the lining of the kiln becomes so thickly glazed that re-bricking becomes necessary. The process is *not* suitable for electric kilns and requires expert advice before it is attempted.

SOME GLAZE DEFECTS. A good glaze should fit its ceramic body and so increase the mechanical strength of the finished pot. Its coefficient of expansion, therefore must be near to that of the body over the whole cooling range of temperatures. While certain faults may be turned to advantage in decorative ware, utilitarian pots require glazes to be technically sound if only for hygienic reasons. It is usually easier to adapt the glaze to match the body but it is important to remember when new bodies are used that results with well-tried glazes may be quite different.

Crazing. This occurs when the glaze contracts more than the body. It is best remedied by first firing the biscuit to a higher temperature and if this still proves unsatisfactory, the silica content of the glaze can be slightly increased. The addition of 5% borax in the glaze could also help. In stoneware, because the body is impervious, this defect may not be regarded unfavourably and can occur because the particular glaze has been over-fired. Re-firing to about 30° C. lower in temperature may well correct this and produce a less shiny surface.

Crackle. In stoneware this can be brought about deliberately by over-firing to produce crazing. The once-fired glaze can then be rubbed with colouring oxide and re-fired to this lower temperature to produce a sound glaze with an interesting net-work pattern.

65

Peeling occurs when the body contracts more than the glaze to cause it to lift off. Its cure may be achieved by a lower biscuit firing or a decrease in the silica content of the glaze.

Crawling usually begins in the early stages of glost firing as the kiln is warming up. In drying out, the glaze shrinks and cracks so that on fusing, bare patches of biscuit and blobs of glaze result. Gum tragacanth or arabic, which burn away on firing, can be added to the glaze to give it more adhesion to the biscuit but the most usual cause is dust particles or powdered oxide on the biscuit. Long standing biscuit or glass-papered pots therefore should be carefully cleaned of dust, and the addition of a little gum to colouring oxides will prevent an excess of loose oxide on the biscuit surface prior to glazing. It is also important to avoid handling biscuit ware otherwise greasy marks may repel the glaze.

Glaze recipes. These were at one time jealously guarded by glazers as they still are in industry today. Some starting point is required but the thickness of the glaze dip, the type of clay body, the source of the raw materials, the type of kiln and the method of firing and cooling will each play an important part in the behaviour of any glaze recipe. A recipe, therefore, is best regarded as a guide and mention of two glazes might indicate how they can best be used.

Harrison's JC481 is a good general purpose leadless transparent glaze which matures at about 1100° C. It can be made to fit many bodies by temperature change alone so that if after their application, as is customary with clear earthenware glazes, crazing occurs, a rise of 20° C. or so will very likely correct the fault. To make a matt glaze it can be used in the following recipe: JC481 – 7: china clay – 1: whiting – 2. It may happen that at 1100° C. a white body will craze slightly while a red body will prove satisfactory. The addition of 5% of iron could be added to maintain the matt quality but provide a sufficient increase in fluxing power to overcome the crazing, though this addition would colour the glaze brown.

A standard recipe for a stoneware wood ash glaze maturing at about cone 8 is felspar – 2: wood ash – 2: ball clay – 1. The source of the ash supply is a variable factor and if after testing at cone 8 the glaze is too shiny, then an increase of perhaps 10% of clay should prove successful. Ball clay is particularly useful in an ash glaze because it encourages adhesion of the glaze to the body and helps to maintain the suspension of the glaze materials in water. Different quality glazes, however, can be obtained by the substitution of all or part of it by china clay, to give such a recipe as felspar – 2: wood ash – 2: ball clay – 1: china clay – ½. But it is well to remember that the same recipe glaze fired to the same temperature on, for example, Potclays' crank mixture, St. Thomas' Body and buff body will flux less on the most refractory crank mixture and most on the less refractory buff body.

MAKING AND APPLYING GLAZES. Carefully weigh the required ingredients to a total weight of say 3 lbs. and place them in a bowl. Crush up any large pieces and just more than cover the powder with water. If possible allow the powder to soak before brushing it with an inch glue brush through a sieve of 80 to 120 mesh into another bowl. Repeat this sifting four or five times and add a little more water until a creamy texture is obtained. It is most important that all of the ingredients pass through the sieve to maintain the glaze recipe. If left standing, even for a short time, some of the ingredients will settle. Certain wood ashes are particularly prone to this and can be held in suspension better by the addition of a few pinches of amisol or a very little bentonite or gum tragacanth. It is most important that the glaze is very well stirred before use, otherwise the recipe will, in effect, be altered and unexpected and inexplicable results may occur. The porosity of biscuit makes possible any of the following methods for applying glaze.

Dipping. This is the best method if sufficient glaze is available. The pot is held firmly but with as little contact with the hands as possible, and immersed in the glaze to coat both the inside and outside. Wire extensions to the fingers can reduce the contact between finger and pot. The pot is then removed, held upside down to empty out the surplus glaze and with a deft twist set upright on a bench. Where handling 'misses' have occured, a finger dipped into the glaze is held vertically just to touch (not stroke) the bare patch and so allow a small blob of glaze (which can later be rubbed smooth) to cover it. Unless ware is to be 'stilted' in the kiln (p. 73) the base must be very thoroughly cleaned of glaze with a damp sponge. If dry glaze is scraped and the resulting powder blown off, the atmosphere soon becomes laden with injurious dust.

Pouring. This method is much favoured for thicker coatings of glaze. The well-stirred glaze is transferred to a jug and then carefully poured into the pot. Immediately, the pot is tilted horizontally and rotated until the whole of the inside is covered. The glaze is then poured back into the bowl. Any drip of glaze on the outside is best sponged off at once. A bowl is now placed on a banding wheel and the pot inverted on two strips of wood or angle aluminium placed across the bowl. The base of the pot is then held by the left hand which turns the pot as glaze is freely poured from a jug. According to the thickness of the glaze and aesthetic requirements, a second or third revolution can be made to increase the thickness of glaze on the pot. If the base of the pot allows of holding by the left hand the stick method is best dispensed with. The wrist is then turned fully in one direction and as the glaze is poured, rotated fully in the other direction and back again to allow the entire surface to be evenly covered. When different glazes are required for the inside and the outside of a pot, the inside is best glazed by pouring, and the outside is then glazed by dipping or pouring. In certain cases glazes can be brushed or sponged onto a pot but this method does not permit of a uniform coating of glaze.

Spraying. This is useful specially for 'green' clay forms, but unless an efficient spraying booth with extractor fan is available, it can be very unhygienic to use.

Tiger-skin textures. Interesting tiger-skin textures can be produced by coating a pot with two layers of glaze by pouring, dipping or spraying. Using a dip of tin glaze either under or over a coloured glaze produces a mottled effect. Variations occur according to the thickness of each dip of glaze and the total amount of glaze present.

CHAPTER NINE

KILNS AND FIRING

The kiln is essential to pottery. Not only does it enable the clay to be converted into its new material but it also is the source of so much of the aesthetic excitement that its technical control permits. It consists of a chamber in or around which heat is produced to raise its temperature to red and indeed white hot heat. This heat can be provided by electricity, coke, coal, wood, oil or gas, and depending on the fuel employed so will the design of the kiln vary. An explanation of the importance of kiln atmosphere might be helpful in understanding the possibilities that these two categories of fuel offer.

When there is an abundance of oxygen from the air to support combustion the atmosphere in a kiln chamber will be oxidising and any colouring oxides in solution in the molten glaze will give the colour of their highest valency. Thus, iron will give amber to rust red, and copper will give green. The effect on biscuit will be to produce a 'clean body' which is free from carbon and perhaps sulphur which might later be troublesome in the glost firing. A reducing atmosphere obtains when the supply of oxygen is restricted to produce an excess of carbon either by the fuel or by the introduction of some form of carbon in the firing chamber. By way of comparison, if a bunsen burner is allowed a full supply of air, all of the gas will burn, but if no air is available then a long smoky yellow flame is produced so that if a saucer is held over it, a deposit of soot or carbon is formed. At high temperature in the kiln, such carbon takes up oxygen to become carbon monoxide (CO), which is greedy for more oxygen and so converts itself into carbon dioxide (CO_2). When the kiln atmosphere contains no further oxygen, so powerful is the process that oxygen from the molten metals in the solution is 'stolen' to reduce a metal oxide to one of its lower forms, or perhaps even to the metal itself. Iron silicates therefore become celadon green or purplish black, while copper gives the red of cuprous oxide, or as this is not particularly stable at temperature, the red metal itself in colloidal suspension, that is in finely divided particles throughout the glaze. The degree of reduction can be varied and an atmosphere which is on the border of oxidising and slightly reducing is sometimes described as neutral.

An electric kiln is a hollow cube contained within two linings of bricks heated by elements of resistance wire set in the walls and floor of the inside. The bricks that make up the inner lining are known as hot face insulating refractories. They have to withstand the extremely high temperature of the electric elements which may be well over 100 °C. hotter than the kiln atmosphere. Their refractory quality, that is their resistance to melt at a high temperature, is achieved by a high content of alumina. They are light and very porous and hold the heat so well that when the hot face side of

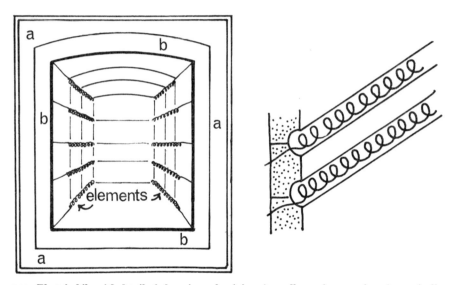

109. Electric kiln with detail of chromium-aluminium-iron alloy resistance wire. a) vermiculite insulating backing-up bricks; b) hot face insulating refractory bricks

a three inch brick is say 1300 °C. the other side is about 900 °C. In order to retain this heat, a brick that is capable of withstanding only 900 °C. and with an even better insulating property is used. These 'backing up' bricks are made from diatomaceous earths or exfoliated vermiculite and they retain the heat to give an outside temperature of about 200 °C. When further insulation is required it is then possible to use a fibre glass type of material.

* see CHAPTER TEN on the making of a small electric kiln

Clearly the better the insulating properties of the materials used the more efficient will be the kiln. The elements become red hot and because the bricks contain masses of still air in their pores, they hold the heat inside the chamber to enable the building up of a very high temperature indeed. A certain amount of ventilation and the 'clean' heat from electricity produce an atmosphere in which there is an adequate supply of oxygen. Because there is no need for a flue and the elements are set inside the firing chamber maximum use is made of the electricity. It is therefore economical to run, and is ideal for pottery requiring 'clean' oxidising atmosphere. As a guide, a one cubic foot chamber requires a 15 amp. power supply, and a two cubic foot chamber a 30 amp. supply. Installation costs for these sizes can usually, therefore be very reasonable but for larger kilns requiring heavier supplies, considerable expense can be incurred. Although certain success at reduction can be achieved by introducing coke, moth balls, small chips of wood, or anthracite into the chamber at from 1100 °C. to 1300 °C., the oxidised coating which forms on the wire is attacked and the life of the element will be greatly shortened. As the elements are very brittle great care is necessary to prevent kiln shelves etc., from touching them. Likewise, glazed pots must be kept well out of possible contact since the glaze at that point would flux with the wire to melt into a metal ceramic mass. When elements need replacing, it is important to see that any such deposit, which can eat deeply into the brick, is carefully removed. Since certain grades of element bricks contain iron which could cause fusion with the wire, it is a good practice to paint the grooves with alumina to act as a barrier. Most electric kilns are controlled by a cooker type of switch which makes and breaks its complete circuit according to the setting. This allows of considerable flexibility of temperature build up. Other electrical devices apart perhaps from exceptional cases are really superfluous. As there is no flue it is important to leave a spy brick or ventilation plug out for the first part of the firing to enable steam, which is injurious to the elements, to escape (fig. 117).

NON-ELECTRIC KILNS

Kilns heated by fuels other than electricity (e.g. coal, fuel oil, wood, gas), can be classified in two ways: those with and without a muffle. If a clean oxidising atmosphere is required then the pots must be completely protected from the flames and gases that these fuels produce. The muffle is a refractory box with one open end for the door. It is set at a critical distance inside its outer lining of firebricks so that the flames pass all round and over it before making their exit through the flue. As with all forms of heating requiring a flue there is a considerable loss of efficiency from the escaping heat. On the other hand the cost of a particular fuel must be an important consideration. The great advantage of using these fuels however is the

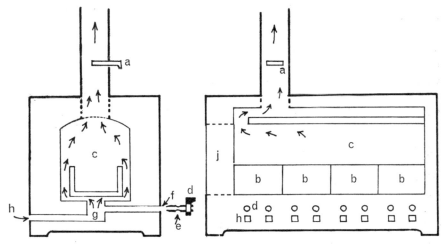

110. Gas fired kiln, elevation and side elevation.

(a) damper; (b) bag wall; (c) semi muffle; (d) gas burner (S);
(e) first primary air; (f) second primary air;
(g) combustion chamber; (h) secondary air preheated
on entering combustion chamber; (j) kiln door

exciting quality of high temperature pottery, both stoneware and porcelain, that they can easily provide when a semi-muffle kiln is used. In such a kiln the flames lap around the pots which are protected from the fiercest blast of the flames by a low 'bag' wall. There must be ample provision for air to be sucked into the flames for complete combustion and where, through the design, this is not achieved, the ware produced will always be at least partly reduced. This is not an ideal condition for oxidised glost earthenware but can produce bodies and glazed work of exceptional interest at high temperatures. The control of the atmosphere is usually effectively obtained by the simple process of adjusting the flue damper. In a kiln with a flue, the movement of air can produce unpredictable results which can be influenced by the weather and the arrangement of the pots within the kiln. In anti-cyclonic conditions there is more 'pull' to the flames which tend therefore to suck in more oxygen.

72

The speed at which the flames lick the pots can be locally increased by a venturi action: that is a faster movement produced by the flames passing through a funnel-shaped space or a space constricted by the shapes of the

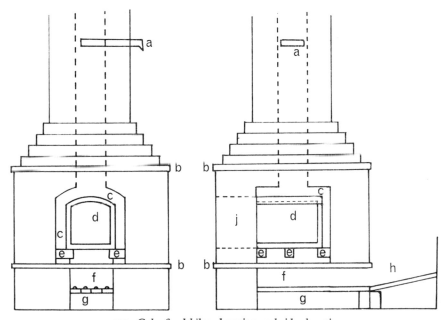

III. Coke fired kiln; elevation and side elevation.
(a) damper; (b) iron clamps; (c) flue space; (d) muffle
supporting bricks; (f) fire; (g) air; (h) preheating fire;
(j) kiln door

neighbouring pots. Especially at high temperatures, volatilised metals can be taken with the flames to 'flash' onto the sides of other pots. Copper and chrome are particularly prone to this and need using with care to avoid unwelcome 'blushing' on other ware. Such are but a few of the hazards that beset the making of reduced stoneware pottery.

KILN FURNITURE

This consists of various items, made of very refractory materials, that are used for stacking pots within a kiln. Shelves, or bats, should be half an inch all round smaller than the kiln floor for satisfactory heat circulation. They need to be thick enough not to warp when subjected to the highest required temperature. The larger they are the thicker they must be or else more adequately supported. This support is supplied by 'props' of various designs and for small kilns the domed and recessed one-inch

  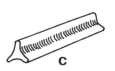

112. Kiln furniture:
(a) stilt for base of glost pot; (b) thimble with base
for stacking plates or tiles; (c) saddle bar for
large bases; (d) castellated interlocking shelf
support; (e) domed end recessed shelf support

diameter and the interlocking castellated types are most suitable. For supporting pots on bats there are porcelain stilts, spurs or saddle bars, and for stacking plates, thimbles and spurs can be used.

BISCUIT FIRING

Clay ware for biscuit firing must be dry before it is packed or 'loaded' into the kiln. Care must be taken to arrange the shelf props, preferably at three points, in vertical columns, so that they are supported through to the floor of the kiln. Pots can be stacked carefully upon each other but particular care must be taken with flat dishes or tiles to avoid warping. Undoubtedly the best biscuit temperature for earthenware is above the glost firing, say 1120 °C. depending upon the clay. For many shapes however, this demands the bedding of ware in 'placing sand'. For many studio pottery centres this labour is not possible so that there is a case for biscuiting at between 900 °C. and 1000 °C. to be followed by a glost firing of 1120 °C. For stoneware the 900 °C. biscuit is generally preferable as it is sufficient to make the ware strong enough to be handled and porous enough to take up a dip of thick glaze. Uniformity of biscuit temperature within a pottery establishment is desirable to produce a uniformly porous body so as to correspond with the particular standard of glaze consistency in use. Having loaded the ware for biscuiting, it is essential to leave some opening in the kiln during the 'pre-heating' for the steam to escape. A low temperature over a period of several hours according to the size of the kiln is necessary to ensure that the steam from the added water is gently driven off. If the firing is too rapid at this stage, the steam might well expand so fast as to explode the ware. When this period is completed, the heating can be increased a little at about two hourly intervals until a dull red heat is visible. It is now that the chemically combined water is driven off. Then the spy hole can be closed and according to the capability of the

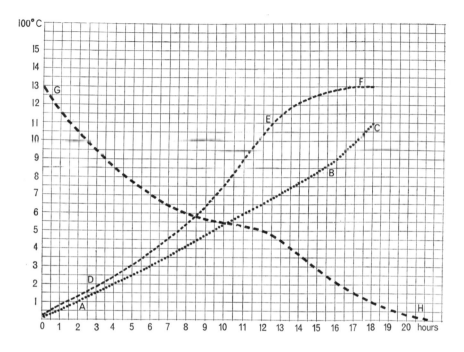

FIRING AND COOLING CHART

AB. Stoneware biscuit firing 0°C.—950°C.
AC. Earthenware biscuit firing 0°C.—1050°C.
DE. Earthenware glost firing 0°C.—1100°C.
DF. Stoneware glost firing 0°C.—1300°C.

kiln, full power can be used if necessary. For 900 °C. biscuit many kilns will not require to be run at full capacity, and it is better to fire cautiously to obtain good quality ware. Again, cooling must be undertaken with care and if ventilating bricks are removed to speed this process they are best taken out at red heat. The critical temperatures are at 570 °C., 200 °C., and 130 °C. when silica in the clay body changes its crystalline structure. Slow cooling is necessary at these temperatures for the molecular re-shuffle to take place without 'dunting' or cracking the ware.

75

For the glost firing, each piece must be packed separately otherwise the molten glazes will fuse together. Pots should be fired separately from their lids, or providing the contact areas are wiped scrupulously clean of glaze, they can be fired with lids *in situ*. In this way the lid retains its shape and the great heat inside the pot (a kiln within a kiln) and the slower cooling is more likely to produce some interesting results. To prevent pots sticking to shelves either their bases must be wiped clean or, if thinly glazed, stilts can be used for support. For vitreous stoneware stilts are rarely used. Unglazed bases of earthenware, however, increase the chance of porosity and eventual crazing therefore must be taken into account. If stilts are used for thickly glazed bases they become embedded and so are difficult to tap off and grinding becomes necessary. It is a good practice to sprinkle a layer of alumina onto the shelves before placing such pots into the kiln to guard them against the possibility of glaze running off the pots. Should this occur, the pot and shelf can then be more easily and successfully dealt with. Care must be taken that sand is not allowed to fall onto the ware below. The warming up of the kiln, as for biscuit, is best undertaken carefully since the raw glaze on a pot near to an element or flame might otherwise crack to produce crawling if dried out too quickly. After a couple of hours the spy bricks can be inserted and the power can then be increased until red heat appears. If necessary full power can then be used.

The required heat of a kiln is indicated either by a pyrometer or cones. The pyrometer consists of an electric thermocouple which projects into the kiln to record the temperature, at that point, on a dial outside the kiln. While it is a useful instrument as a guide for heating and cooling, it does not give the complete information that the potter wants to know. The maturing of a body or a glaze depends upon the amount of heat-work done upon it. It is a function of both the temperature achieved and length of time that it is held that contribute to this maturation. The cones and similar devices were designed to do just this. They are 2 inches high

113. Cone and triple cone socket

triangular pyramids of compressed glaze materials of an exact recipe that they melt and bend over when conditions in the kiln dictate. They are related to a temperature according to the number stamped on them, these being available at 20 °C. intervals. Thus 010 is equivalent to 900 °C, 1 to 1100 °C as per table below. (American cone numbers are similar but do not correspond exactly with cones made in England.) Each cone is pressed into a wad of clay or a cone socket and positioned in the kiln so that it can be sighted through a spy hole. Even if a pyrometer be used, it is advisable to place cones in various strategic positions in the kiln to

cone number	squatting temperature in degrees centigrade		
022	600		just shows red
018	710		clay changes to pottery
014	815		lustres, enamels and gilding
010	900		stoneware biscuit
05	1,000		
04	1,020		
03	1,040		earthenware glazes
02	1,060		
01	1,080		
1	1,100		
2	1,120		earthenware biscuit
6	1,200		salt glaze
8	1,250		
9	1,280		stoneware
10	1,300		bone china biscuit
11	1,320		porcelain
14	1,410		

SOME SEGER CONES

discover how they behave. No kiln provides an absolutely evenly distributed heat and the cones will indicate hotter or cooler areas so that use can be made of this knowledge to give a higher or lower firing to pots as necessary.

The cooling of a glost kiln requires even more care than does a biscuit kiln, if ware is not to be dunted or glazes crazed. If an electric kiln is kept sealed during cooling the effects of a high temperature neutral atmosphere can be better maintained by preventing an inflow of aerial oxygen. With a gas or flue kiln the closing of the damper will diminish the effect of aerial oxygen on the molten glaze, and so might well change the final appearance of the glaze.

From this brief account of kilns and firing perhaps something of the excitement of this final process in the making of a pot can be seen. Although specially at high temperatures the kiln can produce unexpectedly kind and unkind results, yet with experience and skilful judgment the potter always eagerly awaits the drawing of his kiln which is the final arbiter of his technical efforts.

CHAPTER TEN*

MAKING A SMALL ELECTRIC KILN

SPECIFICATION: 1 CUBIC FOOT CAPACITY, 10½ in. x 10½ in. x 13½ in. HIGH
3½ KW. FROM A 15 AMP. SUPPLY

MAXIMUM TEMPERATURE 1,300ºC. AFTER 20 HOURS
FIRING

This kiln was first built in 1955 and, after continuous use with frequent cone 9 firings, needed relining ten years later. Reliable commercial kilns at attractive prices have since been marketed but there is much satisfaction from firing work in a kiln of one's own building. Not only does it cost less than a similar commercial kiln, but it is much more convenient to maintain. Its construction, however, does demand care and like most practical ventures undertaken for the first time, may well take longer to complete than a first glance might suggest.

It is operated from a 15 amp. power supply but it is essential that the connection from the supply to the kiln is made by a qualified electrician and that any requirements of the local electricity board are satisfied.

The stand is made from 1½ in. by 1½ in. 'Handy Angle' cut to size and bolted together with the angle plates provided. It consists of four legs each 48 in. long, four lower bracing pieces each 23 in. long, the base frame made of four connecting pieces and two central bracing pieces each 23 in. long, and a top frame of four pieces 23¼ in. long. A sheet of 14 s.w.g. mild steel, 22½ in. by 22½ in. is used for the base plate.

Building procedure. Two kinds of bricks are used. Hot face insulating alumina refractories, grade 28 (i.e. capable of withstanding approximately 2800 °F. or 1550 °C.) are used for the inside lining and insulating bricks of vermiculite for the outside. A special air-setting cement is used for bonding.

1). Construct the frame except for the top.

* see also CHAPTER NINE

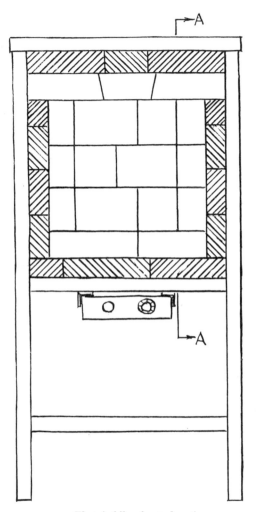

114. Electric kiln: front elevation

2). Place the base plate in position.

3). Cut and shape the element bricks. It will be noted from the drawing details that the grooves for each course differ. An old marking gauge may be used to mark the parallel lines. The bricks, which are very friable, are easily worked with ordinary wood-working tools, but discarded machine hacksaw blades about 12 in. long and $\frac{3}{8}$ in. diameter wood rasps are particularly suitable. The grooves for each 9 in. brick require extending for $1\frac{1}{2}$ in. into a front or back brick as shown in the drawing.

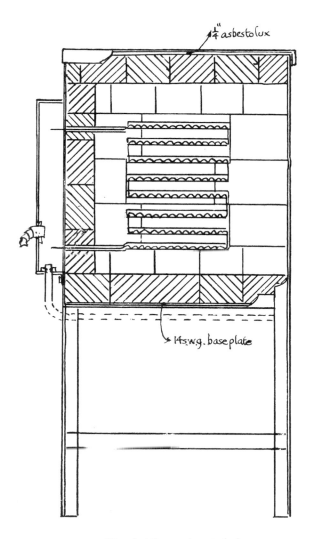

115. Electric kiln: section at A-A

4). Before laying a course, cut bricks where necessary to size and test each course dry. Remove the bricks and lay them out systematically for correct assembly positioning when cementing. The arrangement of outside bricks must wherever possible cover the joins of the inside lining in order to produce a maximum heat seal. Exit holes for the elements can be 'drilled' by persuading a piece of $\frac{1}{4}$ in. rod by rotating and

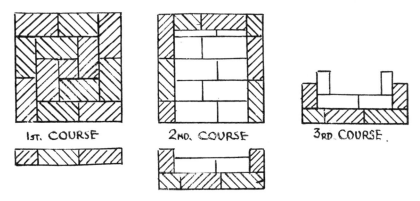

116. *Electric kiln: brick courses*

pushing through the brick. Such rods can be left in position for later removal where the holes occur at cement joints.

5). Mix the cement with water to a creamy consistency and wet the joining faces with water. 'Butter' the surface to give a joint of not more than $\frac{1}{16}$ in.

6). Align the brick with a straight edge and press it firmly into position.

7). Continue course by course.

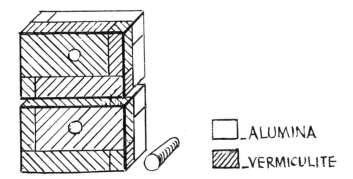

117. *Electric kiln: door with spy holes and plug*

8). The door can be made in one piece or two halves as shown in the drawing. The bricks are cemented together and spy holes drilled and tapered to size with a file. Suitable plugs about 7 in. long are cut and filed from alumina brick. The roof bricks are best cut a little oversize so that their bevelled edges can be rubbed together to make a perfect join. This can be achieved by placing a long brick vertically in a vice (between two pieces of wood to save damage) and rubbing the upper brick's surface with a circular movement against it. Alignment is checked with a straight edge. Slight unevenness of surfaces can be smoothed true by rubbing with a small piece of brick. Asbestolux sheets $\frac{1}{4}$ in. thick are cut for the two sides and top, and positioned after the brickwork has been allowed to dry out for a week or so. The top frame is then fixed.

The elements are made from 16 s.w.g. Kanthal A 1 resistance wire. It is important that the exact length of 43 ft. is cut for each element (for 240 volt supply). The wire is close wound on a $\frac{3}{8}$ in. diameter, 24 in. long iron rod fixed in a vice to incline upwards at its free end. Although the wire is annealed and readily bends, it might be helpful to wear a thin leather

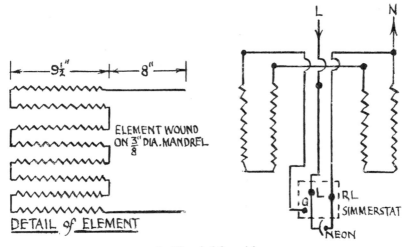

118. *Electric kiln: wiring*

glove on the winding hand. Start and finish 8 in. from the ends of each 8 legged element and leave 2 in. uncoiled between each leg. Count about 40 turns for each leg. When coiled, each leg is stretched to 9 in. and with round nosed or cloth covered pliers bend the element to shape. Care must always be taken neither to scratch the element wire nor to bend it back on itself. The element is fitted by inserting the top and bottom ends through the exit holes and stretching one pair of legs at a time to enable its straight end to slot into the end groove of the element brick.

Wiring. Use 15 amp. asbestos covered wire throughout. The two elements are connected in series at the top by means of 15 amp. single porcelain connectors. Leads **G, L** and **RL** are led through a 1 in. diameter conduit fixed to a base plate bracing angle iron, to the simmerstat and neon warning light connections at the front of the kiln. A metal box is made to fit between the base plate bracings to allow the lamp holder and simmerstat to be mounted. The kiln must be earthed.

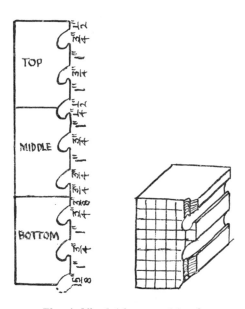

119. Electric kiln: bricks grooved for elements

MATERIALS REQUIRED

Morlite 28 grade bricks, 9 in. x $4\frac{1}{2}$ in. x 3 in.	50
K.I.P. Victor 20 vermiculite bricks, 9 in. x $4\frac{1}{2}$ in. x 3 in. ..	60
Tri-Mor Airsetting Cement	$\frac{1}{2}$ cwt.
Handy Angle and plates	44 ft.
Kanthal A 1 resistance wire 16 s.w.g.	$1\frac{1}{2}$ lbs.
Asbestolux sheets 23 in. x 23 in. x $\frac{1}{4}$ in.	3
Mild steel sheet 14 s.w.g., $22\frac{1}{2}$ in. x $22\frac{1}{2}$ in. (for base plate)	1
X.P.M. (thin), 30 in. x 24 in. (for back cover)	
Simmerstat type TYC (state voltage), neon lamp 240 V., B.C.,	

15 amp. switch-socket and plug
5 of the 15 amp. porcelain connectors
3 ft. of 1 in. conduit, 1 in. inspection elbow, 1 in. back nut,
2 of the 1 in. brass female bushes, and 15 amp. asbestos covered
   wire.

SUPPLIERS

Morgan Refractories Ltd., Neston, Cheshire
Kingscliffe Insulating Products Ltd., Loxley, near Sheffield
Handy Angle Ltd., Uxbridge Road, Hayes End, Middx.
Hall and Pickles Ltd., Bilton House, Uxbridge Road, London, W.5.

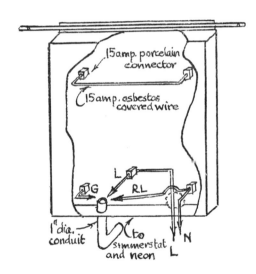

120. Electric kiln: layout wires etc.

CHAPTER ELEVEN

ENAMEL DECORATION

Enamel decoration in its various forms is perhaps more akin to industrial than studio pottery. It is a very fascinating process and allows of effects quite different from other methods of ceramic decoration. It consists of applying to an already glost fired surface a highly fluxed pigment which thereafter melts at a very low temperature of about 750 °C., and fuses into the surface of the softened glaze. Such a low fusing temperature enables the production of very bright colours and the melting of very thin layers of colloidal gold and silver into the surface of the glaze. Unlike other forms of ceramic colour which dissolve into the molten glaze or are covered by the glaze, enamelling is of a much less permanent nature, and frequent handling after some years can cause a notable erosion of the pigment. Since to achieve certain colours a very strict control of temperature is required, highly specialised industrial potteries may fire the ware several times to satisfy the requirements of particular pigments.

It is imperative that ware to be decorated be free from water otherwise the firing may produce a blistered surface. If old glazed earthenware is used, it is advisable to re-fire it to ensure that any moisture, that may have been absorbed through the slightest craze, has been driven off. Bone china, being vitreous, is not subject to this hazard.

Groundlaying is a form of enamelling which provides a flat and uniformly even coloured ground surface that can be patterned readily by scratching through to the smooth glazed surface with the point of a wooden meat skewer. The yielding of the groundlay to the point provides a peculiarly pleasant control and, like scraper board, very fine texturing indeed can be achieved. The ground surface is made by dusting pigment onto an oil base and scrupulous cleanliness and a warm dust free atmosphere are needed for good results. A thoroughly even coating of oil is applied to the ware as follows: pour a tablespoon of groundlaying oil with one or two teaspoonsful of genuine turpentine into a saucer and with a 1 in. soft haired varnish brush mix them thoroughly together by strongly working the brush backwards and forwards in the lower half of the tilted saucer.

The mixture must be sufficiently fluid to allow the brush, moving freely in every direction, to apply an even covering to the ware. It is important to avoid the use of excessive turpentine otherwise the oil covered surface, which is allowed to stand for about fifteen minutes, will dry out too quickly. A pad or 'boss' is then used to produce the necessary even ground surface. It is made by teasing out a piece of cotton wool and wrapping it tightly in a piece of pure silk which is tied to make a firm but resilient pad about 2 in. in diameter. A clean cup is useful to house the boss when not in use. The boss is then dipped lightly in the mixture and firmly padded out on a spare glazed tile until it starts to 'pluck'. Firm, even and overlapping blows are then made with the boss on the tacky oiled ware which is then ready for colouring. The colour is usually applied by taking plenty up on a piece of cotton wool and very lightly dusting it with a circular movement over the surface of the ware. For plates and tiles the colour can be brushed through a 200 mesh colour sieve held a few inches above the ware. Surplus loose colour is carefully removed by the circular movement of a clean piece of cotton wool. The thumb can be run round to clean the edges of pots, and areas of colour can be removed with cotton wool after the shape has been outlined with a point.

Ground resist consists of painting a pattern or an area where colour is not required, with a mixture of black treacle and vermilion tube water colour. Having dried out, the ware is then groundlaid and allowed to harden for twelve hours or so. The ware is then plunged into cold water which softens the painted areas and allows them to be washed off without harming the groundlay colour.

Gold and silver lustre resist. This gives a white pattern on a metalled ground. A pattern is painted with vermilion tube water colour which is very thickly applied and the ware is painted with a gold or silver preparation. Liquid bright gold for example is a finely divided suspension of colloidal gold in a pitch base. If necessary it can be judiciously thinned by adding a drop of petrol. Although only a very thin coating of the precious metal is used, it is economical and more satisfactory to mix it in a gold shell – a glass covered dish made especially for this purpose. After firing the resist will polish off bringing with it some lustre and so revealing the white pattern.

Enamel painting. This is a straightforward process which although it calls for deft brush strokes permits some correction by allowing a mistake to be wiped out with cotton wool. Special brushes are useful for this work and are made up in various shapes known as 'liners', 'tracers' and 'banders'. Good work demands a thorough preparation of the pigment. The colour is passed through a 200 mesh sieve and a little placed on a tile and mixed by means of a palette knife and a very little turps. A small amount of fat oil which dries very quickly, is placed beside the ground colour. The oil and colour are then mixed in small amounts and applied to the ware. Thin lines of gold can be applied simply by banding on liquid bright gold.

The firing of enamel on glaze decoration necessitates a well ventilated kiln to enable the oil fumes to escape, and a well ventilated kiln room to avoid discomfort from obnoxious fumes.

Groundlay and enamel wares are fired to about 750°C. to 800°C. and lustres to about 720°C. Most kilns will reach these temperatures very quickly but for good results a slow firing is needed with a temperature rise of 60 degrees per hour. White glazed tiles are very suitable for early practice, then any white industrial earthenware or bone china ware providing it is absolutely clean can be used. Handmade tin-glazed ware, specially when on a smooth body, is also suitable for any of these on glaze enamel techniques.

CHAPTER TWELVE

SOME RANDOM EXPERIMENTS

As experience is gained in the pottery process, especially in the controlling of various types of kilns, it is inevitable that the observance of chance happenings will encourage experiments with local and specific interests that drive home forcibly some basic ceramic truth. The following are random examples of this kind of experience that indicate yet another fascinating aspect of the craft of pottery.

The Roman experiment. A young enthusiast of the local history society volunteered the information that the Romans made pottery in Joyden's Wood, Bexley, noted for its prehistoric dene holes. Accordingly he brought along some fragments of Roman pots together with some yellowish clay from the same site. The fragments were terracotta red on the outside with a black centre layer – known to archeological excavators as Roman 'liquorice allsorts' pottery. The black, which can also occur on the outside, is due to the reducing atmosphere of the smoky wood fire. The sample of clay was soaked in water, the stones and large impurities removed and then the slurry was sieved through a No. 80 mesh lawn to make a slip. This was dried out on a plaster slab and prepared into a lump of plastic clay. Two other local clays, one from a garden and the other a bluish coloured clay from a river, were similarly prepared and a small bowl was thrown from each sample. A fragment of Roman pot was placed in the Joyden's Wood clay bowl and the three placed close together in the kiln and fired in an oxidising atmosphere to 1,000 °C. On cooling, the three biscuit pots were different from each other in both texture and colour but the fragment had lost its black layer and was identical in colour and texture to the Joyden's Wood sample. This not only reinforced the theory that pottery had been made in Joyden's Wood from the clay to hand but it also indicated clearly that different local clays will burn to different colours when fired at exactly the same temperature in the same kiln atmosphere. The 'blue' clay fired red because its dark colour in the clay state derived from iron in the ferrous form which, with an abundance of oxygen in the firing process, changed to the rust ferric colour. The importance of placing the three samples in the same part of the kiln was emphasized later by firing another similar bowl to 1,100 °C. This changed to a much deeper colour.

'Blue slipper' glaze. The blue slipper clay from the Isle of Wight is notorious for causing disastrous landslides which erode the south coast of the island. A sample of this clay from Blackgang Chine was prepared as above and a shallow test bowl thrown. After firing to 900 °C. a pleasant orange biscuit pot emerged and caused notable surprise by the high pitch of its ring when tapped with the finger. The inside was painted with copper, tin glazed and fired to 1,100 °C. On cooling the walls of the bowl had completely collapsed and squatted on the shelf. The glaze was exceptionally well matured and the body, a khaki colour, was very dense and revealed a slight sheen. Carefully placing the tongue to the broken body there was no suction at all: the body was non porous and vitrified. Since such vitrification was produced at 1,100 °C. it was reasonable to suppose that at 1,300 °C. it might flux into a molten glass. Accordingly the following experiment was carried out. A strip of clay 3 in. x ½ in. x ⅛ in. was dried and biscuited to 900 °C. A one-inch piece of this orange coloured biscuit was broken off and the remaining piece fired to 1100 °C. An inch of this dense khaki body was broken off and the remaining piece placed on a piece of broken kiln shelf and fired to 1,300 °C. On cooling the one inch sample had melted to cover the piece of shelf as a dark brown glaze with an interesting orange peel quality. That glaze can thus be made from certain natural clays strikingly illustrates the mere chemical fact that glaze and clay are composed of similar materials. Perhaps too, it gives more meaning, for example, to the importance in ceramics of felspar which when naturally decomposed produces clay and yet is often used as a main constituent in high temperature glazes. For glazed pottery is the product of heat treated rocks. Again, the surprising high resonant pitch of the 900 °C. biscuit and the vitrification of the 1,100 °C. body are interesting in relation to porcelain and bone china. The latter not only have a high ring because of their customary thinness but because their body is thoroughly dense from their near glassy quality. That a clay should become vitrified at so low a temperature is also useful when attempting to define the family to which a piece of pottery belongs – whether earthen-ware or stoneware. Potters would regard this blue slipper ware as earthen-ware in spite of its vitrified body because it is not capable of permitting high temperature glazes with their peculiar quality, while pottery fired

to 1,300 °C. would be regarded as stoneware even if, as can occur, its body is porous.

This particular experiment provided yet another point of interest since the broken section of the 1,100 °C. fired glazed pot showed clearly a very dark line between the glaze and the body. Accordingly a thin sectional chip was placed under a school microscope which revealed the merging of three distinct layers made up of the body, the body and the glaze, and the outer glaze thus demonstrating the way in which a glaze unites with the body and the effect of the dark intermediate layer (or layers) on the final colour appearance of the pot. Furthermore each layer was seen to contain a multitudinous number of air pockets, a feature not always appreciated, and one of particular interest in such a well vitrified body and such a well matured glaze.

'Playground glass'. The erection of new buildings necessitated the digging of a school playground to a depth of about ten feet. At this level a stratum of pure sand was struck and the following experiment was carried out to demonstrate the common knowledge that glass can be made from sand. One part of the sand was mixed with two parts of red lead in one biscuit bowl and one part of sand was mixed with three parts of borax in another bowl. Copper oxide was lightly sprinkled over each mixture, the pots fired to 1,000 °C. and on cooling a solid mass of glass had formed inside each bowl. The copper developed a green colour in the lead glaze and a turquoise in the borax glaze. Thus not only was it proved that glass can be made out of common sand but that the same metal can behave differently according to the type of glaze in which it is melted.

'Nutty slack' pottery. When coal was difficult to buy just after the last war, an unrationed surface coal was made available in certain parts of the country. It was of a very inferior quality indeed and frequently contained masses of dark grey clayey material. Such a piece was washed and sieved and used to make a pot. Not all of the coal dust had been removed so that an interesting speckled buff body resulted. The experiment, while fascinating at the time, also emphasised the ubiquity of the potter's basic material, clay.

'Lava pottery'. When the floor and bag walls of a semi-muffle gas kiln required replacing, it was found that a cone holder and a three inch bat support, both made of refractory material, had fallen into the combustion chamber. When a temperature of 1,300 °C. is reached inside a muffle

it may well be that the temperature where the air and gas combust is around 1,600 °C. Such a temperature was sufficient to cause these refractories to melt into a glassy matrix similar to the lava from an erupting volcano. A clay made refractory by a high content of alumina is regarded generally to be beyond such behaviour under normal conditions so that the effect of this exceptional temperature on such a clay is a powerful reminder that ultimately all rocks and metals will melt. It is perhaps interesting to note that while no single metal or clay will withstand the extremely high kinetic temperatures that a space capsule develops by friction on re-entering the earth's atmosphere, only partial fusion of the capsule's heat shield takes place because of the combined use of metal and alumina. For not only has alumina a high melting point, but, unlike metals, it is also a poor conductor of heat. Thus this highly sophisticated use of clay in combination with metals, metal ceramics, is playing an increasingly important role in this technological age.

GLOSSARY OF SOME USEFUL TERMS

AMORPHOUS—'without form'—lack of crystalline structure (*see* SOLID SOLUTION).

AMPHOTERIC—that part of a glaze composition, alumina, that is neither acid nor basic.

BAG WALL—a low wall in an open fired kiln that protects ware from the direct heat of the flames.

BAT—a refractory shelf for the kiln; a piece of flat plaster or board on which damp pots are placed to dry to leather hardness.

BISCUIT (*bisque*)—clay that has been burnt to make unglazed, porous pottery.

BULLER'S RINGS—trial rings which contract radially during firing and according to their subsequent measurements on a gauge indicate the work done by heat.

COLLARING—the process in throwing that causes a cylinder to narrow as in making the neck of a bottle.

CONE—a pyramid of triangular tapering section made of compressed glaze materials indicating work done by heat in the kiln.

CRACKLE—a network of cracks in stoneware glazes sometimes deliberately contrived for decorative effect, especially when oxides are rubbed in and the pot re-fired to heal the glaze.

CRAZE—a glaze defect in earthenware. The cracks produce a non-water-tight body.

CRYSTALLISATION—the decorative formation of crystals which develops as a molten glaze cools. Slow cooling promotes this particularly from 850 °C. to 700 °C.

DEFLOCCULANT—a material (waterglass) added to a very thick clay slip to greatly increase fluidity.

DEVITRIFICATION—the crystallisation of an amorphous glaze on cooling.

DUNT—cracking of ware in the kiln through stresses set up in cooling. Often produced by a blast of cold air.

93

EUTECTIC—the percentage composition of two or more materials in a mixture that gives the lowest melting point. Thus 10% alumina (M.Pt. 2,070 °C.) and 90% silica (M.Pt. 1,710 °C.) together melt at the eutectic point of 1,545° C.

EARTHENWARE—glazed pottery whose body is porous.

ENGOBE—a coating of slip.

FAT CLAY—a very plastic clay.

FETTLE—the trimming and cleaning up of clay shapes.

FLUX—a material that promotes fusion of a glaze, e.g., lead, potash, lime.

FRIT—a fused mixture of silica and soluble alkalines or lead. The melt is shattered by pouring into cold water and ground to produce an insoluble, and in the case of lead, a non-poisonous soft glass.

FUSIBLE CLAY—one that collapses at about 1,100 °C. and melts into a glass at about 1,250 °C. (*see* page 89).

GLOST—glazed ware.

GLOST FIRING—glaze firing.

GREEN WARE—clay shapes prior to firing.

GROG—ground biscuit of varying degrees of coarseness. When added to a clay body it 'opens' it up.

KAOLIN—china clay.

KILN FURNITURE—various refractory items which are necessary for packing ware into kilns, e.g. bats, props, stilts.

LAWN—a sieve of phosphor bronze mesh.

MATURE—to develop a glaze or body to its fullest strength (*see* SOAK).

MATRIX—the molten mass of glaze materials in which the glaze is developed.

MUFFLE—a refractory chamber or kiln lining which protects ware completely from the fire.

OXIDATION—the atmosphere in a kiln with an abundance of oxygen.

PORCELAIN—dense vitrified body which is usually translucent when thin and has a particularly high 'ring' when struck.

PROPS—refractory kiln shelf supports of various designs (*see* page 73).

PUGMILL—a clay mixing machine which delivers solid coils of prepared clay, either horizontally or vertically.

PYROMETER—an instrument that indicates the temperature of one area within a kiln.

PYROSCOPE—a material device for assessing the firing conditions within a kiln (*see* BULLER'S RINGS, CONES, TRIALS). An optical pyroscope may be used to assess kiln temperature by a study of the colour within a kiln, e.g. 'red heat'.

RAW GLAZE—i. a glaze made from natural or raw materials (*see* page 64). ii. to glaze in its green state and fire once.

REDUCTION—the atmosphere in a kiln which is starved of a full supply of oxygen (*see* page 69).

REFRACTORY—material that stands up to and resists fusibility at high temperatures.

SGRAFFITO—a scratched pattern made on the clay or through a clay slip or glaze.

SINTER—the fusing together of the body materials as in stoneware and porcelain.

SLIP—an even creamy mixture of clay and water.

SPIRALLING—preparation of clay by folding in a spiral movement (*see* page 13).

SLURRY—a sloppy unsieved clay, usually 'waste' clay left over from throwing.

SOLID SOLUTION—not only when molten but after quick cooling, glaze often remains as a 'solution' in that it develops no orderly pattern that is necessary for crystallisation.

SOAK—the period of firing when the temperature is held steady to allow the glaze to mature.

SPIT OUT—blistering in on-glaze enamel ware due to absorption of water in an earthenware body that is old (*see* page 85).

STILTS—triangular three pointed refractory supports for glazed ware that pevent the glaze from sticking to the kiln bat.

STONEWARE—high fired pottery whose body is watertight, although not always so (*see* pages 57, 89).

TERRACOTTA—'burnt earth', unglazed porous biscuit, often unglazed sculpture made from clay.

THIMBLES—interlocking refractory supports used in three columns to stack flat ware (*see* page 73).

TOOTH—the texture of a clay body gained by the addition of sand or grog.

TRIALS—pieces of the same body and glaze as is being fired, placed in the kiln to allow of easy withdrawal as a check on firing progress

WEDGING—preparing clay by cutting and slamming in a specific manner (*see* page 14).

MATERIALS AND EQUIPMENT

In recent years potters' merchants have developed very comprehensive services for studio and school potters. This is a welcome feature but perhaps calls for particular care when making first orders if the temptation of glossy catalogues is to be avoided and personal or public money is to be spent effectively. Initial equipment can be expensive but the basic materials required are few and comparatively cheap so that if properly directed, the running cost of a pottery compares favourably with that of other crafts. In connection with expense it is well to bear in mind three points. First, the cost of fuel for firing; second, the 'hidden' charges for carriage, especially high in the case of clay; third, the favourable rates offered for quantity supply.

MATERIALS

Before ordering it is important to decide on the scope of work envisaged, such as the type of pottery to be made and the techniques to be employed. It is desirable to develop from a simple start for, if chaos is not to ensue, the simultaneous running of many techniques in a pottery class requires considerable organising capacity on the part of the teacher and a ready co-operation from the students. To this end, the labelling of all materials, whether in stock or in use, is imperative. When stoneware and earthenware bodies are used it is desirable, although not always possible, to keep them separate. If only earthenware is made the earthenware bodies should be purchased since their lower maturing points will favour a denser body and a better fitting glaze. The following is a suggested first list of materials.

10 cwts. plastic clay, buff or ivory. This keeps well in customary polythene bags or wrapping.

1 cwt. powdered clay as above for slip making.

5 cwts. plastic red clay: 1 cwt. red powdered clay.

1 cwt. 'T' material—up to 10% added to above gives an 'open body' for modelling or tile-making.

1 cwt. plaster for moulds and a plaster slab for drying out wet clay.

96

4 lb. red iron oxide.

1 lb. black iron oxide.

4 lb. manganese dioxide.

4 lb. copper carbonate.

1 lb. grey cobalt oxide.

1 lb. chromium oxide.

1 cwt. transparent glaze to match clays: JC 481 from Harrison & Sons is a good general purpose glaze.

1 cwt. Zirconium opaque white glaze—Podmore's SO5.

4 lb. tin oxide.

7 lb. alumina for dusting kiln bats and for glost firing.

For stoneware glazes, 28 lb. each of the following:

China clay, ball clay (powdered), cornish stone, felspar, flint, dolomite and whiting. Wood ash is best collected from local tree-felling sites and washed and sifted in the pottery.

EQUIPMENT

The kiln. This is the most important item and requires to be chosen with great care. Electric kilns are the most convenient to operate and to install and are comparatively cheap to run. The electricity supply available must be considered for when the firing chamber is much over 2 cubic feet, the usual 15 and 30 amp. points will not be adequate. The amount and size of work will influence the choice but it is well to remember that a frequent firing cycle is most desirable and too large a kiln not only mitigates against this but also takes longer to load. Furthermore, element repairs and general kiln maintenance are considerably increased. Two smaller kilns, therefore, may well serve better than one large kiln. Even if a 2 cubic feet kiln is ordered and is subsequently found to be inadequate, it will still be of great use for experiments and in helping a faster turn round of work. The shape of the chamber is important and recently a higher rather than deeper shape in small kilns has been marketed which is preferable for general work. Where a choice exists it is advisable to order the high temperature models with as few 'gadgets' as are necessary for safety. There is little need for a pyrometer on a small kiln.

Kiln furniture. This must be chosen to suit the firing chamber and again, high temperature bats and props, in spite of their higher cost, are recommended. Bats must be $\frac{1}{2}$ in., smaller all round than the ground floor of the kiln, not only to allow for expansion and possible slight movement of chamber walls, but also to allow a satisfactory circulation of heat. Domed and recessed props take up a minimum of space and are particularly suitable for small kilns.

A pugmill is useful for the studio potter and most desirable for class pottery. Clay is placed in the mill's hopper and cut and mixed by revolving half propeller shaped blades so that gradually the clay is moved through a tapered barrel which progressively reduces the diameter of the extruded clay (e.g. from 4 inch to 2 inch diameter). In this way most of the air is expelled to give an homogeneous coil of clay. Suitable pugmills are made with 2 in., $2\frac{1}{2}$ in., and 3 in. diameter outlets and deliver clay either horizontally or vertically. The 3 inch vertical mills are very heavy indeed and require to be bolted onto a very solid wall. The 2 inch and $2\frac{1}{2}$ inch horizontal mills are generally adequate and easily installed. In practice, the optional force lever is essential to speed the delivery of the clay. Hand-operated mills are not recommended.

Banding wheels. These are most useful for coiled pot making and modelling as well as for banding-on slip or colour. They are usually made with detachable heads so that care must be taken to support the base when moved. With the heavy models it is advisable to turn a groove in the spindle so that a set screw, tapped into the other section, can be fitted to allow for free rotation yet prevent the two parts from falling apart.

Throwing wheels. These can be operated by foot or by an electric motor. There are very many types of each and choice is largely a personal matter. Some models have seats, and others are operated whilst standing. Before ordering it is well worthwhile to try out as many types as possible.

Sundry equipment. This will include bins or containers for storing clay, 6 in. diameter plastic lotion bowls for water; Turkey or synthetic sponges; 28 lb. enamel bins for raw materials; enamel or polythene pails or large bowls for mixed glazes; 4 pt. enamel jugs for pouring glazes; 8 inch lawns of 30 and 60 mesh for clay; 8 inch lawns of 80 and 120 mesh for glazes; lawn or one inch glue brushes; a set of scales to weigh up to 7 lbs.; 12 inch calipers; a 6 inch bench carborundum grindstone for grinding bases of pots.

SUPPLIERS OF EQUIPMENT AND MATERIALS

United Kingdom

Potclays Ltd., Copeland Street, Stoke-on-Trent (clays).

W. Podmore & Sons Ltd., Shelton, Stoke-on-Trent (clays, raw materials, oxides, wheels, pugmills, general supplies).

Fulham Pottery, 210 Kings Road, London, S.W.6 (clays, wheels, kilns).

Cromartie Kilns Ltd., Dividy Road, Longton, Stoke-on-Trent (oil and electric kilns).

Acme Marls, Hanley, Stoke-on-Trent (kiln furniture).

Gosling and Gatensbury, Hanley, Stoke-on-Trent (pugmills).

W. Boulton & Co., Burslem, Stoke-on-Trent (pugmills).

Coupe Tidman & Co., Pontypridd, Glamorgan (market two stoneware/ porcelain bodies which fire pure white: 'T' material contains coarse grog; '313 body' smooth clay without coarse grog).

U.S.A.

United Clay Mines Corp., 101 Oakland Street, Trenton 6, N.J. (clays).

Stewart Clay Co. Inc., 133 Mulberry Street, New York (clays).

A.D. Alpine Inc., 353 Coral Circle, El Segundo, Cal 90245 (kilns, etc.).

Electric Kilns Mftrg. Co., Chester 11, Pa.

Denver Pure Clay Co., Denver, Colorado.

American Art Clay Co., 4717 West 16th Street, Indianopolis 24, Ind.

House of Ceramics, 2481 Matthews Avenue, Memphis, Tenn.

Milligan Hardware & Supply Co., 115 E 5th Street, E. Liverpool, Ohio (tools, etc.).

Ferro Corp., 214 Northfield Road, Bedford, Ohio (tools, etc.).

Ohio Ceramic Supply Co. Inc., Box 630, Kent, Ohio 44240 (tools, etc.).

International Engineering Inc., Dayton, 1, Ohio (pugmills).

SOME EXAMPLES OF PERIOD AND MODERN WORK
Figures 121 to 165

These examples have been chosen to indicate various ways in which potters, both past and present, have explored the possibilities of their medium. Some knowledge and understanding of past work proves a background and inspiration for present development. A proper use of clay, according to the method employed, comes only with an intimate working experience. All other influences, however strong, are always subordinate to this appreciation and understanding of the material.

It is the material that permits the final form and decoration of a pot, whatever its purpose. Thus, whether a ritual Cylcadic vase, a pre-historic Yorkshire food vessel, or incinerary urn, a Chinese jar or a medieval pitcher, it is the potter's control of his material that makes possible the expression of his aesthetic feelings in the finished work.

These examples of past work with their rich variety of technique and appeal have one factor in common: they each display the potter's integrity. And perhaps this fundamental is worth bearing in mind when assessing the work of modern potters.

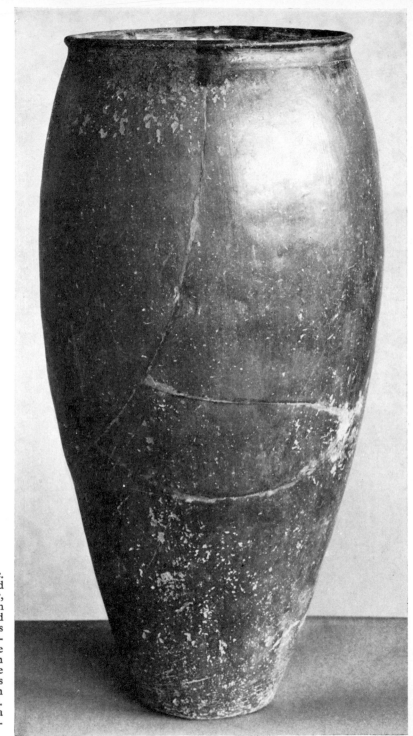

121. EGYPTIAN. *c.* 3500 B.C. Polished red earthenware jar, 52 cm. high with smoke - blackened top. These pots were inverted, partially buried in the ground and fired in bonfire style. The 'black mounth' is due to reduction firing (see p. 69). (courtesy: Victoria and Albert Museum)

122. CYPRIOTE, *c.* 2000 B.C. Polished black earthenware jug, 26½ cm. high, with complex chevron sgraffito decoration (courtesy: Victoria and Albert Museum)

123. CYPRIOTE, *c.* 2000 B.C. Unglazed painted earthenware jug, 25 cm. high (courtesy: Victoria and Albert Museum)

124. MELOS, 2000 B.C. Multiple or cluster vase, probably a ritual libation vessel, with dull black painting on light brown body. Height 34 cm. (courtesy: British Museum)

125. MELOS, 2000 B.C. Jug with beak spout. White slip over brown body, with dull black painting. Height 28 cm. (courtesy: British Museum)

126. CHINESE, *c.* 2000 B.C. Large unglazed earthenware jar with painted decoration. Quantities of these magnificent burial urns (usually about 40 cm. in height) were discovered last century during the construction of trans-continental railways in Northern China. The bold triple scroll pattern in iron brushwork are supposed to relate to ritual dance movements. The Farandole dance known in Provence, is said to have been established by an ancient Greek colony. The snake-like windings executed by the dancers as if moving to the centre of a labyrinth in sympathy with the terrible journey of a dead person threatened by evil powers before reaching his heaven. Another characteristic feature of these urns is the pair of very small down turned handles (courtesy: Victoria and Albert Museum)

127. ENGLISH, Yorkshire. Prehistoric food vessel from Goodmanham. Coiled with richly impressed band patterns. Height 10.5 cm. (courtesy: British Museum)

128. ENGLISH, Berkshire. Prehistoric handled beaker from Abingdon. Height 17.8 cm. (courtesy: British Museum)

129. ENGLISH, Glamorgan. Prehistoric cordoned incinerary urn with string impressed
pattern. Height 37 cm. (courtesy: British Museum)

130. ENGLISH, Middle bronze age. Incinerary urn with collar or overhanging rim, and with string impressed pattern. Height 37 cm. (courtesy: British Museum)

131. RHODES, 1400 B.C. Vase with octopus motif. About 40 cm. high. The dignified proportions of later Greek amphorae are evident in this graceful form which rests on a small but very workmanlike base (courtesy: British Museum)

132. CURIUM, 1200 B.C. Stemmed cup with cuttlefish motif. About 25 cm. high (courtesy: British Museum)

133. CHINA, Chou dynasty, *c.* 1000 B.C. Tripod bowl with lug handles. Height 14.5 cm. (courtesy: British Museum)

134. LAUSATION CULTURE (East European), *c.* 1000 B.C. Urn in pale grey terracotta with vertical fluting and six bosses. Possibly an early example of moulded ornament made by pressure from within the pot. Height 12.5 cm. (courtesy: British Museum)

135. LAUSATION CULTURE (East European), *c.* 1000 B.C. Urn with grooved band decoration.
Height 11.5 cm. (courtesy: British Museum)

136. EGYPTIAN, 50 A.D. (?)
Carrot shaped amphora about
50 cm. high (courtesy: London
Museum)

137. GALLO-ROMANO (Cologne). Unglazed earthenware pot decorated with applied clay rolls (courtesy: Victoria and Albert Museum)

138. ROMAN (?), c. A.D. 3. Beaker, about 14 cm. high (courtesy: London Museum)

139. CHINESE, Sung dynasty (860-1269 A.D.) glazed stoneware vase 46 cm. high. The vertical runs of glaze emphasise the powerful upward thrust of the throwing ridges. The sensuous elegance of this pot is very different from the classical (intellectual) concepts of beauty favoured by the potters of Ancient Greece of c. 600 B.C. (courtesy: Victoria and Albert Museum)

140. PERU, Tiahuanaco. Double spouted stirrup vase painted in red and white slips, height 16 cm. Similar vessels, with whistles in the spouts, were partially filled with water and carried by herdsmen who relieved the monotony of their vigils with the melodic notes produced when these vessels were gently swung backwards and forwards at arm's length (courtesy: British Museum)

141. MEXICAN Olla ware, with incised pattern. Height 20 cm. (courtesy: British Museum)

142. KOREAN, 12th century. Porcelainous celadon bowl, diameter 19.5 cm. The incised decoration takes up more glaze to give a soft emphasis. The term celadon derives from a French novel *L'Astrée*. Celadon glazes were probably made to imitate the characteristic colours of jade (courtesy: Victoria and Albert Museum)

143. ENGLISH, 13th century. Thrown jug of galena glazed earthenware with combed decoration and 'thumbed' base. Such jugs would be ideal in inns for *carrying* ale or wine up a flight of stairs from a cellar. For *pouring* from such a jug one hand would be needed for support near the base of the jug on the side opposite to the handle. Table jugs which are designed more specifically for pouring require handles set nearer to the centre of gravity, as well as more prominent spouts (cf. figs, 125, 146). Found near the Royal Exchange, London (courtesy: Guildhall Museum, London)

144. ENGLISH, 13th century. Red earthenware jug, 37 cm. high, painted with white slip. Found in Basinghall Street, London (courtesy: Guildhall Museum, London)

145. ENGLISH, 13th century. Earthenware pitcher, 43 cm. high, with sprigged decoration and 'thumbed' foot. Found in Southwark, London (courtesy: London Museum)

146. ENGLISH, 14th century. Earthenware pitcher with parrot-beak spout. Sprigged decoration under a yellow glaze. Similar spouts are a feature of jugs made at this time in the Bordeaux region of France: this similarity may have resulted from the enormous wine trade with England at this period (courtesy: London Museum)

147. ENGLISH, 15th century. Earthenware watering pot with holes in base. Decorated with free brush strokes in white slip, beautifully calligraphic in quality. A feature of this pot is that the wide rim serves as a handle (courtesy: Guildhall Museum, London)

148. ITALIAN (Florence), 15th century. Maiolica dish, 44 cm. diameter, painted in green and purple on tin glaze (courtesy: Victoria and Albert Museum)

149. ITALIAN (Florence), Maiolica jug, 24 cm. high, freely painted brush work in green and purple on tin glaze (courtesy: Victoria and Albert Museum)

150. PERSIAN, 16th century. Tin-glazed pot painted in blue and black on the glaze. Height 29 cm. The use of tin oxide to opacify an earthenware glaze was discovered by the Arabs in the 10th century, and became widespread in imitation of Chinese porcelain (courtesy: Victoria and Albert Museum)

151. GERMAN, 16th century. Salt-glazed stoneware with mottled brown glaze over sprigged decoration (sprig moulded leaves and coiled stems). 33 cm. high. The mask or face on these large bottles is said to be an effigy of Cardinal Bellarmine who was resented for his persecution of the Protestants in the Low Countries (courtesy: Victoria and Albert Museum)

152. ENGLISH, 17th century. Slip-trailed dish by Thomas Toft, diameter 44 cm. These Staffordshire dishes are outstanding for the draughtsmanship and vigorous designs by peasant craftsmen working in a community unaffected by the later ideals of the 18th century whether Chinese or Neo-Classic (courtesy: Victoria and Albert Museum)

153. PAUL BARRON. Two jugs with respectively fingered and brushed slip (courtesy: Victoria and Albert Museum)

154. MICHAEL CARDEW. Black glazed earthenware cider jar with cut glaze decoration (courtesy: Victoria and Albert Museum)

155. BERNARD LEACH. White porcelain fruit bowl. Diameter 28 cm. (photo.: St. Ives Ltd.)

156. BERNARD LEACH. Tall stoneware bottle, brush work in iron over white slip. Height 35 cm. (photo.: Pottery Quarterly)

157. WILLIAM STAITE MURRAY.
Stoneware long-neck bottle
(courtesy: Victoria and Albert
Museum

158. ANN WYNN REEVES. Dish and bowl (courtesy: Victoria and Albert Museum)

159. LUCIE RIE. Tall-necked bottle, and bowl (courtesy: Victoria and Albert Museum)

160. IAN AULD. Slab-built pot with applied rough slip and incised decoration. Stoneware with dry glaze. Height 56 cm.

161. IAN AULD. Slab-built pot in stoneware with dry ochre glaze. Height 45 cm. (photo.: John Minshall)

162. GRAHAM BURR. Oxidised stoneware pot, 15 cm. high, oatmeal coloured ash glaze
(photo.: Brian Shuel)

163. GRAHAM BURR. Slab-built pot with cross fluted façade. Unglazed stoneware, washed with vanadium (photo.: G. W. Watkinson)

164. GRAHAM BURR. Slab-built double curved pot in dipped and poured glazes, 31 cm. x 27 cm., oxidised stoneware, 1280°C.

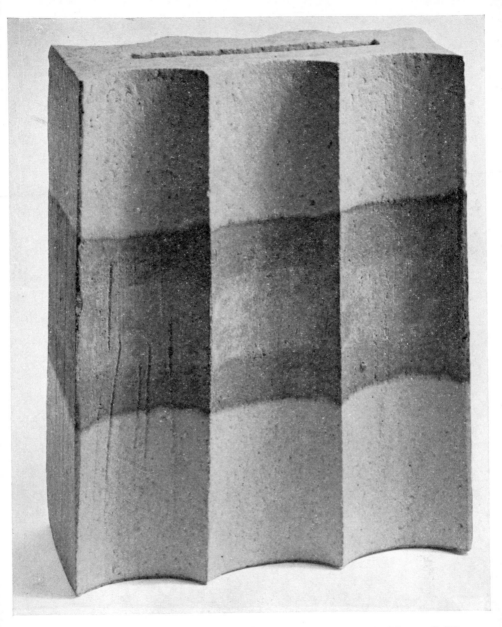

165. GRAHAM BURR. Slab-built stoneware pot with vertical fluted façade (photo.: G. W. Watkinson)